LIFE AN

A Retrospective Collection

by

The Manchester Irish Writers

to Celebrate Thirty Years

of their Creative Word Journey

1994 – 2024

Edited by Kevin McMahon

Cover Design by Emma Jackson

SCRÍBhneOIRÍ

Dedicated to the memory of departed members whose creativity, honesty and friendship have enriched our lives.

Ar dheis Dé go raibh a n-anamacha

CONTENTS

Editor's Foreword

Moss
The Way Back
Selfie Mode
Possibly Venice
Night Boat
Christmas 1978
The Light from Here
Reunion
In The Big House
The Last House
Last Thing

Rhythmic Footsteps
The Last Tinges
Morning Moon
Nature's Matinee
Bullets and Bus Tickets
Stack of Rifles
Silencing Silver

EDITOR'S FOREWORD

In 1994, author Alrene Hughes was commissioned to run a series of workshops for aspiring Irish writers, by Commonword, based at its Manchester office. Rose Morris was one of the attendees, and, when the programme finished, at the end of its funding period, she asked if Alrene would continue with the workshops, relocating to the Irish World Heritage Centre, in Cheetham Hill. Initially, this would be supported by Commonword, with access to workshops led by Mary Dorcey. As there was clearly an appetite among participants to continue, the move was made – and the Manchester Irish Writers' Group was formed.

Alrene and Rose nurtured the group – most of whom had not previously written anything for public consumption = providing a safe and friendly atmosphere for constructive advice and critique. I am sure that few in those early days would have imagined that the group would still be flourishing thirty years later. The volume of work produced over that period has been immense, and the group has benefited from the skills of each individual member over the years. Many members have progressed to publish internationally best-selling work, achieve professional performance or win numerous accolades and awards, being selected for publication by some of the most prestigious titles in the U.K., Ireland and beyond. However, there has never been any trace of elitism or exclusivity: the novice writer is still made as welcome as the professional, and entitled to the same level of support, scrutiny and advice.

The Manchester Irish Writers comprise a disparate group: some born in Ireland; some second or third generation immigrant descendants; some with little Irish connection, except a desire to learn about, explore and celebrate Irish culture. The unifying bond is a passion for writing and a desire to learn.

The thirty years have marked some tumultuous times for the relationship between the U.K and Ireland. The Good Friday Peace Agreement ended thirty years of bloody conflict, much of which carnage was witnessed first-hand by some of our members. A decade of commemoration saw us remember the centenaries of the First World War, the Easter Rising, the War of Independence and the Civil War, all of which featured in presentations staged by the Manchester Irish Writers' Group. The Nobel Prize awarded to the Irish poet Seamus Heaney was celebrated by the group, as his death was mourned. Fr Eugene Dolan – a lifelong friend of the poet, from their time as classmates in St Columb's College in Derry – joined is in commemorating Heaney in a moving tribute.

Of focus is not, however, confined to our spiritual home in Ireland. As a Manchester collective, the horror of mass murder in the Arena bombing prompted us to respond as writers do – by writing.

Our members have benefited from opportunities that would be largely inaccessible to individual writers, such as the chance to perform monologues at the Royal Exchange Theatre, in 2004, when our *Drawing Breath* collection was launched. Through a series of publications from our own publishing company – *Scribhneoiri* – our writers have been able to see their work in print, many for the first time. The calibre of that work is exemplified by the stature of celebrities who launched the collections. Our first publication, *At the End of the Rodden* (1997), enjoyed the support of actor and director Aine Moynihan (founder of An Lab Theatre, Dingle), and writer and broadcaster Polly Devlin OBE launched our collection of poetry, *The Retting Dam*, in 2001. With director Louise Twomey, and Newfound Theatre, a showcase performance was staged at Manchester's Library Theatre in 2007.

Our twentieth anniversary saw us publish a celebration of two hundred years of Irish immigration to the city, with the *Changing Skies* monologues performed in front of sell-out audiences at the Irish World Heritage Centre, by a team of professional director (Hellen Kirby) and actors, courtesy of a Lottery-funded grant, secured by Alrene and Rose. On a smaller scale, there have been regular performances staged by the Manchester Irish Writers where members have had the opportunity to read their work to very appreciative audiences, often supported by our friends in fellow cultural groups, such as the Claddagh Association of Irish Dance and the St Wilfrid's Comhaltas Ceoltoiri Eireann musicians.

More recently, coronavirus prevented our supportive meetings, and hindered public performances, but the writers threw themselves into the world of remote meetings to ensure that, in those trying months of being closed in our homes, a creative outlet was still available.

The quality of work produced by a small group – very rarely numbering more that fifteen at any time in its history – has been phenomenal, as I hope this small cross-section will testify. Whether in poetry, short story, memoir, reportage, drama or novel, each writer has developed a mature and unique voice – each paying tribute to the value of the group in aiding their development. At the same time, the group members have developed the experience and critical vocabulary to enable detailed and constructive criticism, rather than a bland acceptance of the first draft of any of our work. This has been honed at times in our history by invaluable support and coaching by locally based academics, such as Professors Liam Harte and John McAuliffe. The value placed on membership of the group is evident from the reflections tendered by writers alongside their contributions to this retrospective collection.

The longevity of the Manchester Irish Writers' group, like the quality of its output, is a testimony to the hard work and vision of its founders, Rose Morris and Alrene Hughes. After thirty years, the group is, I believe, as strong as ever, and well placed to continue to produce writing of the highest merit, and to encourage many more novice writers to commit to print.

It has been a remarkable privilege to edit this collection, and I hope its readers will appreciate it equally. However, the greater honour is to have been able to count myself a member of this quite extraordinary group. I hope you enjoy this sample of our work, and that many of you reading this will be encouraged to join our special group.

Kevin McMahon

February 2024

BARBARA AHERNE

Barbara joined Manchester Irish writers about 2015. Her first piece of writing prior to that was for the book *Irish Manchester,* by Alan Keegan. She decided to join Manchester Irish Writers hoping to improve her writing skills, and she has appreciated receiving invaluable advice from other members. Barbara enjoys writing about personal experiences and recollections, and those passed down by her family.

LEAVING HOME

Chris was born in Croom, County Limerick in 1942. He was the youngest boy in a family of ten, eight boys and two girls. One sister was older than him and the other sister was younger. The cottage they lived in was next to the railway on the Old Mill Road, Churchtown, Newcastle West. There were fields surrounding the cottage and there was a level crossing. The nearest neighbour was on the other side of the crossing.

He was always expected to accompany the girls home in the evenings if they went out anywhere, even though he was quite young. They all rode bicycles into town and returning home. He was particularly interested in horses and was keen to become a jockey.

The trainer wanted to bring him to England to train as a jockey but his mother refused to let him come. He was fourteen years old and about 1957 He went missing. His parents had everyone out looking for him including the Garda Siochana. They did not find him, but found his bicycle tied to a tree on the banks of the Shannon. His parents must have been frantic with worry by that time, as there were only four or five siblings still living at home. The guards decided to drag the river but nothing was found. He travelled around working for farmers trying to earn enough money to live on.

He eventually worked his way across Ireland and actually worked in Maynooth college kitchens under an assumed name. About 1963 he left Maynooth and got on a ferry to England intending to go to his brother Dan in Nottingham, but got on the wrong train and ended up in Manchester, where he met me in St. Brendan's club in Old Trafford. He lived in digs just around the corner from the club. He worked in the building trade as he was a joiner by trade. He asked me for a date, and we started going out. After a while I found out he had not contacted his parents in the six years since he had left.

My mother and I encouraged him to write to them and we all travelled to Ireland to see them in 1964. We had got engaged at the beginning of the year. As we were driving through the Curragh in Kildare, during the early morning, it was quite misty even though it was summer. In the mist a motor cyclist came into view and as he passed, he waved us to stop. Even in the mist he had recognised Chris. He invited us back to his house as he had not seen Chris since they worked in Maynooth. He kept calling Chris Tommy as Chris had used the name Tommy O'Brien. Chris called him on one side and explained that it really was not his name.
His parents were overjoyed to see him return after the long absence. His father, two sisters and one brother came to Manchester for our wedding in the October. His mother would not travel and had never been outside Ireland. We have been to Ireland many times since then and we were together for almost fifty-five years until he died in May. We had always wanted to go and live in Ireland but never had

the chance. We had looked at various properties but always too expensive. So, it was never meant to be.

Author's note: My husband, Chris, was known by the name Christy to his friends and family in Ireland. I wrote this account of the unusual circumstances of his departure from Ireland as a tribute to him.

CABBAGE IN THE KENNEL!

Our youngest child Bridget was born in 1980 and when she was a year old. I returned to work, part time, to cover for someone on sick leave. I eventually stayed on full time as the other member of staff never returned to work. Chris looked after her during the day whilst I was at work, usually returning home at about 2.00pm. He was working nights, and it was difficult for either of us to get enough sleep as Bridget was a very active baby day and night, as had been our eldest daughter.

Just before Bridget started school, she had been round to a friend's house with her daddy to see the new Alsation puppies and of course she wanted one. I protested about this as I was working. However, they went ahead and got the puppy. Bridget could not pronounce the name we wanted for the puppy, so she said, "I am going to call her Sally," so that was the name she got. They rang work to say they had brought the puppy home so I thought they may have forgotten about food for it, so I dashed round the shop getting things that a puppy would need. As it happened the girl who sold the dog had thought of that and gave them some food to take home.

Sally did not like to be alone at nighttime and made a lot of noise, so we had to take her upstairs to bed. That is where she spent every night until she could no longer get up the stairs. When she was a few years older, I used to give her the centre out of a cabbage after I had finished cutting off the part I needed for our meals. She loved to chew at it and played about with it.

One evening Chris came home early from work and went around the back of the house where there was a kennel which he had made for the dog, but, needless to say, she would never go in it even with the soft bedding I put in for her. She was a nosey dog who liked to see everything that was going on, so she used to lie at the front gate, which was padlocked to see all that was going on. After looking in the kennel, Chris came running into the house saying, "Why have you hung a cabbage up in the dog's kennel?"

I replied, "I have not hung anything in the dog's kennel."

He said, "Come and look."

I went around the back and looked into the kennel and sure enough there was something hanging in the kennel suspended from the ceiling. There were wasps flying around it. It was an oblong shape with a colour similar to a cabbage. I said, "That's not a cabbage. It's a wasps' nest."

I rang a friend who kept bees to ask him about the best way to tackle getting rid of it. He told me the best way was to wait until the evening when it would be much cooler, and they would quieten down, as the days had been very sunny and warm. Then we could get it into a black bag and get rid of it. I told Chris what our friend had said, but Chris decided to put woolly socks over his shoes and trouser legs and protection over his face and gloves to protect his hands. I had gone out for the evening.

When I got home Bridget was laughing and told me what had happened. Chris had got a black bin bag and a stick; he held the bag under the nest and gave the nest an almighty whack with the stick. That was a big mistake. The wasps swarmed out of the nest and Chris had to run like mad to get away from them. He did not get stung due to the precautions he had taken, although it could have been a disaster.

OUR GARDEN

Long ago we had no path
Garden was just grass
Rustic fencing at front
Not many plants to show.

Path eventually laid
Led to rear garden
Muddy with rain
Apple tree there

Worked hard on garden
during summer mowed the lawn
made borders with plants.
Planted second apple tree

Lots of apples to make
Apple pies for tea.
Patio laid to reduce size
Swing garden seat table
Chairs and parasol

Summer evenings spent
On sunny days having

Tea outside.

Became a wilderness,
No time to spend on garden
Working every day, raising family
Attending to their needs.

And pastimes, no time for
Other things. Family now grown,
Moved on. Busy with other things.
Gardener came to clear the
Wilderness. Now quite bare
Waiting for renewal.

MARTHA ASHWELL

Martha joined the Manchester Irish Writers in 2014. She was born and educated in Manchester and has worked as a social worker in child-care and in various secretarial and administrative roles in banking, industry and education. She has taken part in numerous voluntary projects and is a qualified counsellor. Martha has three children and eight grandchildren.

Now living in Heaton Mersey, she has written extensively on subjects such as war, migration and peace. Her memoir, *Celia's Secret: A Journey towards Reconciliation* was published in 2015. A short story: *Sights and Sounds,* was included in the anthology: *Something About Home: New Writing on Migration and Belonging,* published in 2017. Her prize-winning poem *The Theatre of War* was published in the *Buzzin Bards: A Manchester Poetry Anthology* in 2019 and *The Happening at Bessbrook*, her debut novel, was published in 2022.

Martha is also a member of the South Manchester Writers' Workshop. In 2021, she joined the Glass Room Poets, which meets monthly at Manchester's Central Library. She is currently writing a series of children's stories in collaboration with her daughter, Clare, and daughter-in-law Nicola. Find out more at http://marthaashwell.co.uk/

EXTRACT FROM *THE HAPPENING AT BESSBROOK*

… He asked Jimmy if he could borrow one of his new carts and without a second's hesitation Jimmy agreed and they brought the little cart home. Paddy cleaned it until it was spotless. They laid fresh straw on the bottom and placed a mattress on top. It was like they were making up a wee bed for me. Mammy watched them from the window and tears came to her eyes as she remembered the cot Daddy had made for Paddy when he was newborn.

'I'd made ready that same cot for all my babies and I loved it still. Aye, don't some things have a value beyond all reason?' she'd said.

Then, they put clean sheets on the mattress and covered it with woollen blankets and thick rugs. The sides of the cart they lined with bolsters, borrowed from Granny and the aunties. Two brand new pillows were set aside to support my head. Slowly, they pushed the cart back to Jimmy's. His old horse, Rafferty, was chosen to pull the precious load from hospital to home for he was as steady as a rock and totally trustworthy.

When they arrived at the infirmary, my condition was unchanged.

'We carried you on a stretcher from your hospital bed, along the dark corridors, down the stone steps and out into the clear fresh air,' Paddy told me. 'Gently, we placed you on the mattress we'd laid down for you. Then we tucked the sheets and blankets under your weak little body and placed the rugs over you for extra warmth and to keep the dampness out. There was a layer of frost nestling on the edges of the cart, which we wiped clean, and the air was milder after the heavy fall of snow and there wasn't a breath of wind. Our own breaths struck the air and trailed behind us as we moved forwards cautiously across the sparkling snow. Jimmy sat aloft and held Rafferty's reins and Daddy and myself walked slowly at either side. 'Twas like a funeral party. As we passed down the streets and lanes, people stood by in complete silence, their heads bowed low. All I was thinking was that this sorrowful journey would bring you home, Evie, to your final resting place before the grave.'

All this time, Mammy'd been waiting anxiously at home. She'd cleaned the house from top to bottom and it was neat as a new pin.

'My heart was pounding,' she said. 'I felt dizzy and my stomach was tied in a dozen knots for I couldn't allow m'self the thought of what lay ahead, And, if I did allow it, I was that feared I could hardly bear it. Kathleen told me I mustn't worry, for all this stress was making me ill. How could I not worry, Evie? I hadn't slept for nights, and I was trying to stay strong for you and for the family. That morning, I didn't know which way to turn and, if it hadn't been for Kathleen and Paddy, I think I would have deserted everyone just to be free of it all.'

Mammy remembered saying: 'Here, John, lay down Evie's mattress ... not too close to the fire now. We'll be quiet as mice but we'll need to carry on our lives as usual.'

That day, like every other, she'd made breakfast and continued to keep the house clean and tidy for she didn't want me breathing in any dust She moved through it all as though in a dream, making bread and preparing the family meals. She followed the advice the doctors had given her; moistening my lips; giving me a few sips of water every hour. One by one, the cool drops trickled down my throat for I couldn't swallow anything at all for myself. I was still passing tiny amounts of urine and Mammy did her best to keep me dry and comfortable.

9

Visits were limited to close family. Of course, Maura came to see me early on with her mother. She'd cried bitterly, so upset she was. Her mother did her best to comfort her but she was heartbroken at the thought of losing me.

It was heartbreaking too for my Daddy and Kathleen and Paddy for, when they left home each day, they didn't know whether they'd find me alive or dead on their return.
Mammy couldn't put her nose outside the door without someone asking about me.

People were very kind. 'I'm so sorry for yous all Mrs O'Dowd,' they'd say.

'Is she any better? Sure to God, she'll get well soon enough.'

'How're ye coping Bridget? 'Tis a worry for you all, so it is.'

Perhaps they were expecting the doctors and nurses at the hospital would make me better. They were shocked and saddened alright when they heard that I'd been brought home to die. No doubt, they were thinking of paying their last respects and of the wake and the funeral to follow.

Fr O'Mahoney and Fr Conner visited too and had many a cup of tea and a chat with Mammy as the long hours passed.

Tears came into Mammy's eyes when she told me: 'They prayed over you, Evie, and blessed you with holy water. I said I'd stay up during that first night and Paddy and Kathleen said they'd share the night-time vigils with me. The night passed very, very slowly and I dozed several times in the big chair by the fire. I thought of the times when I'd to get up for you children when you were babbies. Sometimes, you'd take a long time to settle.

Now I prayed: 'Dear God, don't let Evie die. I don't care how long it takes but please, please don't let her die.' ...

Author's note: The Happening at Bessbrook *was inspired by my visits to Northern Ireland where I learned about my ancestors' dependence on work in the local linen mill. As a member of the Manchester Irish Writers, I received critical appraisal during the reading of passages from this novel. The Manchester Irish Writers offer meetings which have structure and purpose, focusing on the development of writing skills. A nurturing environment is provided where fledgling writers can stretch out and learn from constructive criticism and genuine affirmation. There's such warmth and encouragement among our members; I felt immediately at home, and I value their friendship very much.*

IRISH SOLDIER OF THE SOMME

One rainy day in April 1851 the Duignan family disembarked at Liverpool. They came from a place called Mohill in County Leitrim. Seven of them, there were; some were deathly pale, some had rosy cheeks. The older lads were strong like their Da but the weaker ones, boys and girls, were trailing, touching their Mammy's skirt as it dragged heavily across the cobbled quay.

They settled first in Macclesfield. Maybe the lads found work on the land. Then, on to Manchester where they put down roots and worked their way as best they could. Times

11

were hard and the years passed slowly, long day following long day. They missed Mohill and the people they loved. They missed the green fields and high wind-swept skies.

Generation grew from generation; deaths and births went hand in hand. The natural passing of life and its subsequent renewal affected them just like everyone else. They made friends; some of their own kind, others who were neighbours and church people like themselves. Integration secured them another land to love - England.

In 1898, Tom was born. He was a strong independent lad with an honest face and a bright smile. He loved his family but he craved adventure. Tom hadn't much interest in politics, but he always knew right from wrong. At seventeen and a half he signed up for war. His military induction included a visit back to Ireland, somewhere near Dublin, where he received basic training. As a Catholic, he attended Mass on Sunday with his other Catholic comrades. They had to leave Mass early to avoid the condemnation they received from some of the worshippers who didn't look kindly on any man dressed in British uniform. It hurt Tom to think that he was scorned and despised for doing his duty.

He fought at Ypres and then at the Somme. Tom was shot by a German soldier while fighting to defend a railway station which had been captured by the British side. It was bad, very bad! The bullet just missed Tom's femoral artery. They carried him out to the hospital site dodging the bullets and shells. He'd lost so much blood, they feared he would die but somehow, he managed to cling on. A few weeks later they sent him home, home to England where his family had been praying for his safe return. He became another statistic! Another lie!

Tom recovered and lived on with the effects of his injuries. He limped through the years but maintained his sense of humour and his sense of proportion. He never complained; he had no regrets. He married, and he and his wife raised four children. He trained in accountancy and worked long hours in the city ensuring that his own children were free to make the choices they wanted as they grew up and left the family home. Eventually, eight grandchildren were born, and they were the joy of his life.

Tom was loved for his humour and kindness and for the twinkle in his eye. When he was asked, 'What would you do if you met the soldier who shot you?'

He answered, 'He was probably just a lad like me! I'd kiss the bastard and thank him! Thank him for releasing me from hell on earth. By trying to take it, he gave me my life. If your time's up, it's up! Mine had some way to go. It wasn't the same for all the lads who fought so bravely for King and country. I've no regrets, though! I did what I had to do.'

There's more than a little bit of Ireland in England today. For all the wrongs that have been done, England has provided succour to those who left to escape the hunger, the lack of work, the deprivation of land and inheritance. For the Duignan family the Irish heart remains. The English influences are deep-rooted, and Tom's children and grandchildren have prospered in their adopted country. Yet, there's still a strong and enduring pull to Ireland and the little town of Mohill deep in the Irish countryside.

Author's note: I wrote this piece for the Manchester Irish Writers as a contribution to their theme 1916.

NOLI TIMERE
DO NOT BE AFRAID

I remember the coat that Dada wore
and the boots
that squelched black mud
on long winter walks.

Boldly we strode, hand in hand.
He, a poet; his pen his spade.
Digging for scraps, shaking the soil,
exposing the raw, straggly roots.

We strolled by graveyards
between the mountains and the sea
while I, in youthful innocence,
picked sloes.

We sought familiar places,
remembering relationships,
the intellect and the spirit;
the essence of human life.

The countryside lay littered with debris
as we searched for deeper meaning.
Memories play tricks;
distort the reality of our world.

I frowned upon rifle butt and coffin.
The bog, lay cold beside me, deep and black,
holding its ritual killings,

leaving its mark; a scar on Ireland

But nature heals,
if nature ever fully heals.
My father had seen battlefields
strewn with bodies.

They died where they fell, yet not forgotten.
Barley grows there now, their spirits long
flown.

Drinking sloe gin, I raise my glass
to the woman who bore me,
to the father who raised me.
It flames in the glass, disturbing me, settling
me.

The hefty cobble once thrown in spite
remains an heirloom,
a reminder of those
who chose not to love one another.
The door into the dark reveals shadows.
Our minds are as open as traps!
I listen; I hear and understand
what my father told me.

Noli timere. Do not be afraid.

Author's note: This poem was written as part of a planned Manchester Irish Writers' project and presentation reflecting the work of Seamus Heaney. Unfortunately, the covid pandemic interfered with this plan.

A JOURNEY OF THE HEART: 1935 – 1964

A tall middle-aged man, originating from Northern Ireland, smart in suit and tie, sits at a pub table. He has a glass in one hand and a cigarette in the other. He's thrown his trilby on the adjacent chair. A half-empty whiskey bottle stands on the table. He holds the cigarette towards the palm of his hand to shield it – perhaps from an unseen draft. The date is around 1963. He's in talking mood and reflects with uncharacteristic honesty about his experience of migration.

'Well, there wasn't much left for me in Bessbrook … thirty-two, I was, m' wife and baby dead and me out of work. 'Twas a terrible time I had losing them and I needed to start over. You'll know what I mean? … So, I made plans to join m' brother, Joe, in Manchester. I was looking to get a decent job and send money back home.'

'Things weren't easy for m' mother and father since all us children left home but I'd a feeling there was more to be done with my life than following family into the mill or scratching round for a useless job which was hard to come by anyway. I knew mother'd be glad of the money and I told myself that'd make up for the fact I'd be leaving. Didn't think I'd be homesick, but I was. I missed my sister, Lizzie terrible, as well as the old folk.'

He stubs out his cigarette and takes a mouthful of whiskey.

'But, Manchester's not such a bad place you know. And the parks make up a wee bit for the flowers of summer and the sun shining on the black lake … though it's never the same.'

16

'Sure to God, I've enjoyed the new kind of freedom though; away from the church and the neighbours. People don't know my business and there's no-one to judge you. There's a lot to be said for that alright. But, I'd to adjust to new customs, and I'd a wee bit of trouble making myself understood. I joined with other Irish fellas drinking and talking into the night. We were all missing home, the sweet smells of the country and, Jesus, we even missed the rain, falling as it does in Ireland like no other place.'

'Aye, we missed the comforts, such as they were … and the banter too. I'd to adapt to the new thinking and some attitudes towards us Irish weren't so positive. It made me smile to know they were confusing me with the Paddies. But, on the whole, people were good enough. 'Course, I'd no idea what the future held … how could I? But, I'll tell ye this, I was making the best of it. I'd settle a bit, I thought, and then go back on visits. Aye, I'll go home and things'll be just the same. … But, the fact is things weren't the same; experiences change you and people change; they see the differences when loved ones return … if they ever return.'

'Christ, I've learned to my cost, that migrating is not just a chance to travel or to earn money; no, it's far more than that; it's a journey … a journey of the heart. And sure, crossing the water's just the beginning. … Oh I was full of hope at the start; I'd live with Joe, I'd find a job quick enough. I'd go back and forth and send all manner of letters and packages. Aye, and I know, as you'll know yourself, that for those who leave, a great many stories tell of the journey … but not nearly so many of those left behind. Yet for them, there's often a great sense of loss and a feelin' that it can never be the way it was … never.'

He turns the cigarette packet in his hands and then lights another cigarette.

'Sure, grief's a terrible thing. My mother didn't understand that … Jesus, she didn't. And she fell into a terrible deep depression when I, her youngest, was gone. They tell me she complained of a pain in her heart for which there was no cure, and I just knew from the pain in my own heart … I was part of the cause ... sure, I feel the guilt to this day.'

'I suppose, at first, she'd think I'd make a new life for myself, and I'd be meeting my new wife soon and maybe she'd have more grandchildren. But I know she sensed the loneliness that was in me ….. Sure to God, I could see it in her eyes. And for me, the one who left … oh! I feel it now; the bitter yearning being away from home and craving the comfort of loved ones. Christ, I think leaving was the worst pain; the pain of a broken heart, of a lost homeland; a severance like no other … like you've cut yourself adrift … a detachment … a disconnection. D'you know what I'm saying?'

He takes another drink, filling his mouth and swallowing slowly.

'But we won't talk of that; lingering too long can wound you to the point of distraction. Sometimes, for sure, it's like a death in the family, a great loss; so deep is the sadness at the parting. But, you'll know yourselves that for many, there's simply no choice. Poverty, hunger and no work offer few options but to do your best to help your family. By seeking a better life, you can give something back from a great distance … wherever that may be … I was lucky, so I was. After a few scrappy sales jobs, I got a good job at Renolds working as an engineer.'

'AND, THEN MY LIFE CHANGED when I met Celia. But, she was married and the war came and she couldn't get out of the marriage. ... We had to find a way to be together; we loved each other. Sure, didn't we have FOUR children?' ...
'All this time, they've lived with her and her husband so as they'd never know they weren't part of a 'normal' family. Celia was awful keen on 'respectability.' Aye, it came before everything else to her. ... But, Jesus, they're MINE ... they're MY flesh and blood!'

'But, didn't we decide it'd be for the best? That's what we told ourselves; so they wouldn't be upset. God knows how she got Sam to go along with it; we'd to keep it secret, 'course. How could I ever have agreed to it? God, it's heartbreaking .... so hard.'

He sighs deeply and is close to tears.

'I'd go home twice a year to see family and I was faithful in this 'til my mother died in '56. My father had died a few years earlier. But, with the death of my mother, there was no home to go to anymore. Oh, I'd visit to see other family alright, but, though I'd made a life for myself in England, 'twas a life I'd to hide from my Irish family. Sure, how could I have told my mother she'd four grandchildren in Manchester she'd never see.'

He pours the dregs from the whiskey bottle and lights another cigarette.

'Jesus Christ, I'd a huge burden on my shoulders. I'd to work and support Celia and the children but couldn't claim them as my own. For some years, when the children were

19

young, I even lived with Celia and Sam as a lodger. God knows why we thought that would work. There were awful rows and I realised I'd to leave and get a place of my own.

So, I've lived my life as a bachelor, snatching brief moments with the youngsters; a trip to the park on a Sunday or a bit of shopping in town. It's no wonder I feel so angry and miserable, though I haven't put a name to it. One time, when I'd the winnings from the horses, we went to C&A and I dressed the lot of them in one go.' ...

'Sure to God, they must know how much I drink and they can see for themselves how much I smoke. What do they make of it, I wonder? They'll never find anything out from me in my lifetime, that's for sure. But, my children .....
God help them .... they called me ' uncle'.

'So, that's my story... I'm a man of few words and even fewer explanations. Jesus! I'm not that far from my own death now and I have to face it; I know I've not been as honest as I should've been. There's many things I should've said, things I should've shared ... but nobody asked me the right questions.'

'In the end, you play the cards you're dealt. You do the best you can ... but sometimes you lose the game. Do you know what I mean?'

Author's note: Recently edited, this monologue was performed at the Manchester Irish Writers' performance evening Crossing Over, *which featured poetry, prose and drama relating to displacement and migration. It tells the story of my own father who came over from Ireland in the 1930s. He met my mother, who was in a dysfunctional marriage. They fell in love and went on to have four children. We were all raised in the marital home thinking we were the children of our mother's husband. Years later, I found out that this was not the truth.* This is the basis of my memoir, Celia's Secret: A Journey towards Reconciliation.

THE THEATRE OF WAR

Gunfire moves east away, dark sky, scorched earth sets the scene.
Trees stripped of leaves, stark sculptures against a barren no-man's land.
The Cherry and Aspens are long gone, whilst, I, the lonely soldier battle on.
I act out orders; no case to argue, petty right or wrong.
The stage is set, the script is written but this is no theatre of dreams.

An unknown bird, the lark perhaps, rises from poppy-filled field,
It's song restrained by the bitter sound of clattering guns.
Gone, gone forever are these fields where hay was made.
The sun sets now on fields of death, the landscape naked and exposed.

I think of home, soliloquize to loved ones old and young.
Filthy, not refreshing, is the rain that falls so heavily.
Do not leave my soul among the dead nor let me know decay.
Gunfire, like applause, ceases as curtains close upon this scene of devastation.

In the wings, I wait in joyful hope.

First published in The Buzzin Bards: A Manchester Poetry Anthology *(2019)*

Author's note: The Theatre of War *won the Stockport Garrick Theatre Poetry Competition in 2019. It was inspired by Nick Dear's play,* The Dark Earth and the Light Sky, *which tells the story of the poet Edward Thomas and the American writer Robert Frost during the period leading up to the First World War. Thomas sadly lost his life in that War.*

BRIDIE BREEN

Bridie joined the Manchester Irish Writers' Group over two decades ago, in 2001, having been introduced to founding member Rose Morris at the Irish World Heritage Centre, at one of the group's publications launch, called *The Retting Dam*. Membership of the group has shaped her writing and provided opportunities to collaborate on projects and showcase work over past years. This embrace of creativity is a fresh gift each and every time she is in contact. An added depth is knowing such rich variety of shared heritage possessed by fellow Manchester Irish Writers. *A Stone of the Heart*, *Drawing Breath* and *Changing Skies* are among the many enjoyable projects completed together.

Irish born, Bridie hails from Athlone in Co Westmeath, the town that she still considers as a hearted home, She is connected through the *Poetry in The Park* group there, along with her family and many friends. As a Manchester-matured writer, her adult life has been spent in Prestwich. Children and grandchildren create roots and hold her secure. She believes she is most creative when drawing from the strength of that liminal space that lies between both cultures.

Now retired from her career in Community Psychiatric Nursing, Bridie enjoys reading and writing poetry in all its forms: poetic prose, haiku, short scripts, eco-poetry, voice-overs, short stories and monologues. Media platforms used regularly are Soundcloud and Facebook, with a little Twittering. Poetry forums and open mic performance sessions locally are havens of joy, fun and a great way to appreciate other people's work and support specific charities.

A proud member of Manchester Irish Writers, Bridie has been published in anthologies both national and international over the years. Her writings are a reflection of interest and inspiration spurred by the human condition, migrant voices, injustice, sisterhood, valuing our planet and the multiplicity of topics encountered as life experience moves along. Listening to that inner voice, loving life and gathering the joys of laughter remains a tonic for the heart and soul. Following those ups and downs of a national covid lockdown she is finally collating own publication.

Bridie would like to share some of those moments of collaboration that held meaning and value to her over the years. Remembering particularly all those audience members who joined us to celebrate and commemorate MIW events at The Irish World Heritage Centre, whose heartfelt commentary on resonance felt, always added a richness by sharing their own story of migration.

CHANGING SKIES – REFLECTION

I left Athlone at aged 21 years old. The youngest girl. I left my whole family behind to follow a dream. I wasn't street wise, I was naive and trusting, excited and terrified at the same time thinking of the path in life I was choosing. Well, it was half a choice really. You know that feeling, don't you? When things won't change unless you make it happen. Then you make do, create roots and try to immerse yourself in two lives for a while, the woman who is here in Manchester and the one who wishes inside to be back there in Ireland. All the time there's a constant yearning that doesn't go away. My children have grown now and the mirror reflects how time has passed. Sometimes inside I wish I could have forgotten my roots altogether, not clung so much to my Irish identity. Become more English in nature. Then other times I truly wish I could manage to go back more often, not just in emergencies when someone was ill or to go to a funeral. I never placed priority on my own wishes, I lived to keep my family together through good and bad times. Yet occasionally if truth be known, I would wonder, just wonder, what life might have been like without emigration.

Too long gone, yet the heart beats on
and the spirit within breathes a sigh.
Choices made, as the road of life stretched on.
Now I find the gap too wide.
So, I jump from here to there, as often as I can.

I meander down streets held familiar in my heart.
Strange now, with different faces
Some a shadow of former times
As I glance across the Shannon, feel the breeze in my hair
I wonder how time would have been filled,
if I hadn't gone, over there.

If I stayed, would I have married an Irishman
If I stayed, would success have come my way
Then I remember the struggle for a job, with a future.
The times I cried.
The heartache.
Then I know why I left. I had to leave. I had to try.

No matter where you go, always the faces that can be picked out of a crowd. Well, I for one can pick an Irish man out of a crowd a mile away. I'm not so good with the women, they are far too glamourous, but an Irish man, it's a look, a way of walking, that's before he utters a word. When I say to people I meet, that Manchester has become home to me, I do feel that. I do believe it inside. I look at my adult children and like many here, often went to Heaton Park with them when they were little, glad of the thinking time when they'd be playing. Glad of the time to myself, a chance to soak up memory, surrounded by green fields and space. I don't know if it's just emigrants but the sense of passing time is always close to my mind and feels part of my being and soul.

People often say to me how they find that hard to believe after being in Manchester for over 30 years, that I still sound Irish but you know, even in the bad times, when Manchester was bombed, I was always proud to be me. I just didn't speak a word out loud for a week. Isn't it strange how the word home can be simple or complex?

As an emigrant, I have never lost the sense of exactly who I am and what I am, maybe I think too much about it. I have proud Mancunian children and my only regret is that I didn't steep them more in Irish tradition music and dance, so they can pass it on to their own children.

Perhaps my love of poetry will stay in their veins, perhaps my mother's sense of humour which is part of me, will help them through life too.
Pass it on they say
Language, culture, tradition, stories of olden days
What happens though
When the cracks widen and gaps appear
Which differ between generations
When information isn't desired
When being green on St Patricks day
And dressed as a leprechaun is just fun?

Words are listened to but not heard
A quiet shame is apportioned from young to old

For daring to hold head high
And espouse a time
Where families that prayed together, stayed together
Its successful assimilation, the blending of cultures
As quietly done, as a breath is drawn
And life has moved on.

Sadness cans soak the gaps of the past
But the new generation finds values of its own
Is the past, just the past, with newness ahead
Perhaps what isn't felt in the heart
is best buried as if dead
But the sharing of a smile, now and again
Or a passing glint between migrant eyes who meet
On a St Patrick's day parade on a Manchester Street
Allows the spirit free, permits the Celtic heart to soar
And sure, where's the harm
in trying to pass on, that little bit more.

Author's *note: The* Changing Skies *event at Irish World Heritage Centre culminated in publication in Manchester Irish Writers' anthology in 2014. I still love its cover as much today as I did then. My piece was intended as a voiceover to introduce the evening. Hauntingly beautiful background music of Enya added a poignancy that still gets such positive feedback. It's a piece that will touch the migrant heart, no matter when emigration comes calling. Look it up on* Soundcloud *under my name to enjoy its blend of spoken word and poetry.*

PROCLAMATION FOR ALL

The scroll of proclamation
rolls words off my tongue.
One hundred years on

Easter 1916 bleats from within
the Risen lamb that bled into veins
of the men and women who testified
to the call to rise, to stand united.

A furnace to fire eternal endurance
through the lilt of a freedom song
Each Irish man and woman
Every daughter and son felt the fist of change
It pounded across the land.
Demanding choices to be made
lines to be drawn, sides to divide
and new history to form.

A mere century on from Grattan's demise
the tears of many were shed
Emancipation the sought after prize
Innocents died in the fury
while the raw truth of the cause
forced the iron claw to unfurl
Dominance no longer appeased the masses.

The pulse of men whose hearts
raced as their pens scribed
In a time when signatures sealed their fate
Markers of rebellion, so distinct
they were sought out
to be executed.

History coddled the deep
mourning of generations
The road ahead transformed
beyond belief.
Regimes of colonial past

illuminated by the rising dawn.
Home ruled hands may not have grasped
the essence of Irish hearts
Their entrenched will to change
The question remains, as to where we'd be
if the blood of those in 1916
Became names on a chalked board
Erased out of our imaginings.

Author's note: When the Manchester Irish Writers showcased an evening of work to commemorate the centenary of the Easter Rising 1916 called The Risen Word, *I wrote a series of poems to share on the night. It felt important to remember those gone before. Our history is a complex one, the fight to gain freedom to govern a nation, a difficult path to have trodden. Whilst many of us migrants have made homes here, we may also share different perspectives. Yet, knowing we have more in common than that which sets us apart. This event embraced writers who birthplace across the border gave a different lived experience. Thought provoking and memorable. Available on* Soundcloud.

DRIP DRIP DRIP DADDY

Childhood recall, stands me
a pale skinny legged creature
in a white petticoat.
Awaiting a wash
in a scullery room, before bed.
The Belfast sink, so deep
Its base filled with
a thousand-minute cracks.
Ice cold water flowed to cranium numb.

The draining board creaked
as pestered digits
sought out scattered tools.
Stripy braces pinged
when you bent over too far,
I was more than amused.
A stretch across pursed lips
steeled by an intense stare,
You fiddled with copper piping
Washer missed; vice gripped
both fingers instead, cursed
and muttered every synonym of fool.

A single forehead vein bulged
exerted and enraged
Snaked a path amid perspired droplets,
hinged precariously on bushy eyebrows
above a focussed glare.
I place you, Daddy, centre stage.
Drag you out laughing
from my Pandora's boxed off
cobwebbed brain
Thoughts wash over my sands of time
Solidified now by wiser adult eyes

At seven years old,
a freshly communioned self
I try to recollect it all.
Trudge through
the dense mist of memory
To find the sweet softness
of her smile again.
The Angelus pauses
The decades of Rosary at tea.
Magnificat, recited at six o clock by family

Devotion to the purest
Mother of all mothers
called a halt to the plumbing,
while the labourer knelt in prayer.

At a safe distance
Out of arms reach
I stand shivering
to hover in the doorframe.
Two slender pipes stand anew.
You weave from side to side
Admire the work
Then turn to silently, inspect me
Hair strands sucked
in fretted consideration
I hide, for fear the light behind
flimsy broderie anglaise fabric
can trace my outline, too sheer.

Now, I flashback from time to time
When I run to tighten taps
I choose to exculpate deeds in memoriam
Sage words of my mother philosopher
Mantras embedded so deep in my mind
I still hear her voice instruct
Check carefully whether the good
characteristics, outweigh the bad
And remember
no one is perfect in this life.

Author's note: Poet John McAuliffe, Professor of the School of Arts, Languages & Cultures at University of Manchester ran a series of workshops for Manchester Irish Writers. The collaborative project with him and Dr Liam Harte, Professor of Irish Literature, English and American

31

Studies at University of Manchester included Northern Irish Writers, and resulted in publication of two of my poems in Something About Home: New Writing on Migration and Belonging *(Geography Press), The workshops helped to consolidate ideas, then create work worthy of print, uplifting to unleash creativity inside, a piece written on a prompt in here and now, then have considered feedback. A Poetry Summer School by Carcanet Press in 2022, with John McAuliffe and Michael Schmidt gave joy, learning about the craft of poetry in good company.*

1960s MORNINGS

An army topcoat covered the bed
My arms unable to reach sleeve ends
I snuggled a little longer,
under a rough khaki collar
Brasso-ed lapel buttons
subjected to extra shine
with early morning breath

Expert in the art of getting dressed
underneath mother's makeshift bed
of army layered grey blankets
Her Foxford blue woollen blanket always
well minded in the twin tub.
Two of us to each end of bed,
topped with a light quilted throw over.
Homemade from clothes fabrics long
outgrown
'Always a use if you look' she would say
How right she was.

There was nothing to be done

for the horsehair mattress though
A well-loved relic of bygone
grandfather times.
An instant spike of pain
when least expected
A pincer move required to
pull though a flannelette sheet
Examined, then surgically removed
Countless tiny holes
in candy stripped cotton
waiting for a toe tear
Instant denial and a quick flip
to the other side of the bed

The particular grey light
that shone through curtains
informed of winter.
A corrugated shed roof
glistened as if bejewelled
spoke of richness in imaginings

Artwork on the inside
of the sash window panes
Each one of a dozen small glasses
decorated by Jack Frost
Waited for tiny fingers
to etch and sketch in ice
before the call to breakfast
echoed up the stairs.

Smell of coal fire in the Range
Porridge in the pot
Expedited a fully dressed
eager eight-year-old

for the morning dash below
First place at the table
got the biggest boiled egg
and enough hot water for a wash.

Author's note: A memorable evening performance by Manchester Irish Writers called Echoes of Ireland *sparked memories of childhood in the 1960's. Sometimes all it takes is a quote to get a person thinking. 'You might be poor, your shoes might be broken, but your mind is a palace' (Frank Mc Court in* Angela's Ashes). *Years have a way of slipping by so quickly and even though we fill the time, it usually happenings in close family and friends that evoke the most action to carve a particular path. That's what it been like for past few years now. Embracing a new energy as menopause came and went, inspired a renewed delving into many topics, womanhood, sisterhood, embracing ageing, Irish identity, folklore and Celtic myths and legends of Ireland. It's such a rich tapestry that interweaves with our ordinary lives.*

WEAVING THE TAPESTRY OF LIFE

The weaving tapestry of life from age to age has never stopped.
A scorched scar of divinity remains wreathed into the nature of Irish soul
Stories spun on alchemy, fairy lore and legend
gather threads of every garment that clothed time itself.

Mystics, seers, poets and elders passed tales from then to now
Whispered stories into ears of corn, carried seeds on winds of change
Dreams drifted in smoke swirls of fires lit by Druids,

illumined a portal in mind, sifted the good and bad of
the past

Yet, standing still, in sacred places of the first Gaels,
images soar.
Each millennial compressed sod of turf, holds the spoor
of hunters and prey
Circles of woad inked the skin of Celts, stained as blue
as new age skies
Mere presence transfixes focus, as thoughts traverse to
bygone days.

Freedom fills the air, soaks up fresh awe and power.
Carved memory of lives lived, in each blade of grass
each fertile patch and every milked cow that nurtured
life,
captures long held beliefs in the breaths of the present.

Imaginings of sovereign kinship among Tuatha De
Danaan,
Dagda, the Good-God, a Father to Brigid, retreated to
the underworld
Returned warriors to life, summoned seasons by harp,
a magicked cauldron fed an endless bounty.

Chambered cairns, lying West of Kells, settled on
Loughcrew limestone hills,
Passage tombs, light aligned to rising sun of the winter
solstice,
released souls interred; Sidhe Gaoithe of passing primal
spirits
had offerings made by common folk, for milk yields
and ripe crops to prosper.

Ancient myth of Cailleach Bheara, divine hag of immense proportion.
Our earth Mother, Garavogue, presided over landscape.
She wished to rule all of Ireland, she filled her skirts dropped boulders on land, Carnmore to Loar and Gained Carnbeg.

Her last step faltered, as she leaped from rise to rise
Her wildness ebbed, strength diminished, but not before the human child entering this world, had ability to walk stolen away
Eons of light and dark have shifted, since those many moons and suns ago

In the valley of Rathnew, lies a Hill of long-held charms and mystery.
where a trinity of sister Goddesses Ériu, Banba and Fodla,
wedded Mac Greine, Mac Cuill and Mac Cecht (Sons of Sun, Hazel and Plough),
Allegiance made to sovereign ones at Uisneach, a hallowed place of awakenings.

Lugh, a warrior horseman meets Ériu. Songs sung still echo
"Hail Eiru cupbearer of Lugh, Hail Ériu lover of Amergin
Hail Ériu essence of Ireland". Ériu lies beneath the Catstone
Votive offerings still acknowledge wind, water, earth, fire spirits of life

A gathering of Kings from every province, made laws to keep land and nature

amid druid flames and illumination; An Bother Naofa
forged with the majestic
Hill of Tara and mound of Rathcroghan where Queen
Maeve ruled holds history
Sepulchral cups raised to kings and queens crowned as
mist descends

The battle Goddess Morrigan, transporter between life
and death, shape shifter
Goddess of bird and earth, whose breasts nourish the
living and regenerate the dead,
granted monarchs sovereignty and venerated High
Kings
Water of life gifted, continues to spring in grace and
celebration.

Ritual reminders present at Imbolc, Bealtaine,
Lughnasa and Samhain
Where communioned minds, connect, hold hands aloft
on sacred ground;
Invocations harken those deadened to breath, to relive
as
bodies sway in the gentle breeze and bared feet greet
the new dawn.

*Author's note: Sometimes when planning to take part in an
evening of creative writing with Manchester Irish Writers,
other ideas are generated and new pieces formed.* Weaving
the Tapestry of Life *is one such piece that simmered in
thinking for a while. There is much gratitude felt and
appreciation experienced being part of Manchester Irish
Writers over the years. It goes way beyond words for me.
Here's to the years ahead for us as a group and the ever-
present voices of those poets and writer members who have
gone before us. Never forgotten.*

DES FARRY

Des has been a member of the Irish Writers Group for 10 years, relishing the variety of members who have published or not published; who have been or still are members. This is, he feels, what makes the Manchester Irish Writers' group an interesting and helpful group to be part off, and keeps it fresh, with new ideas. This ensures that it holds and continually attracts new members who can add different viewpoints or suggestions to any text submitted.

BLOODY IRISH NEVER TURN UP ON TIME!

The dry heat in Marbella Old Town really dictated what my wife and I would choose from the Steak House menu. It was a day for salads and cold drinks.

'We'll have a Caprese and a Chicken Caesar Salad, with a large San Miguel for me and a Vodka with Fresh Orange Juice for Kath,' I said to the Spanish Waiter who tapped it into his Tablet.

'Agus an uisce?'

'No, no water,' I replied.

He disappeared back into his restaurant with the menus, returning a few minutes later to place a small Tyrone Red Hand flag in a cork base on the table. 'I recognised the accent,' he said,' So you're one of Mickey's Men fans?'

I nodded and so began our acquaintance in 2015 with one of the most remarkable and unusual men in Gaelic Football. The Spanish waiter was actually an Iraqi engineer from

Baghdad. He is the only Iraqi Gaelic Football Goalkeeper in the world, also the Founder (and sole member) of Baghdad Gaelic Football Club.

'How on earth did you get into Gaelic Football?' I queried.

'Operation Desert Storm, the first Iraqi war in 1991.'

Growing up in a mixed Christian, Muslim and Jewish quarter, Akilles Haider was football mad with teams of boys all chasing, tackling and dribbling through its squares, occasionally crashing into the customers at tables sipping coffee outside of the shops of the old city.

Everybody wanted to be a Pele or a Zinedine Zidane.

He quickly discovered that the best way to get in as many teams and play as many games as possible was to be the goalkeeper … nobody wanted to go in goals, everybody wanted to be a striker.

By 1991 he had started to study engineering at University when his life changed for ever. His father decided that massive change for the worse was about to change their lives, sold his textile business, and moved the family to Surrey in the UK, where Akilles finished his degree and joined the Merchant Navy as a ship engineer.

It was 2003 on his first trip to Ireland after his ship had docked and unloaded its cargo at Galway that Akilles discovered Gaelic Football as he sauntered up from the quays. It was the noise and cheering from the pubs that caught his attention.

Ulster teams had become major contenders in All Ireland competitions with Mickey Harte's Tyrone having started to reinvent Gaelic Football with their blanket defence and possession football.

Armagh had won the 2002 All Ireland and were defending their title against their neighbours Tyrone in the 2003 Final, the first occasion in 114 years that two teams from the same Province had contested the All-Ireland Final.

Akilles managed to squeeze into the Dail pub off Shop Street and experienced top quality Gaelic football for the very first time in his life.

He was immediately hooked by the speed, the scoring, the tackling and tactics of the two Ulster teams as they fought to dominate each other, Armagh to make it two successive Final wins, Tyrone to win their first ever All Ireland.

He immersed himself in Gaelic Football rules, styles of play and resolved to get involved. The opportunity came when his father decided to move the family to the Costa del Sol and get into the restaurant business. Akilles followed, having tired of his seafaring life.

He discovered Costa Gaels Marbella who were looking for players and became their goalie, trainer and tireless promoter. CGM are a mixture of Iraqis (2), Spanish, Aussie/New Zealand players around a core of resident Irish supplemented by passing Ryanair crew and Dunne's Stores staff from the Mijas and Fuengirola outlets.

'The bloody Irish are always late for training!' he grumbled. We met up again with Akilles last week where he was bursting to tell us the latest news.

'CGM had just beaten Gibraltar to win the Spanish GAA Championship and had started a ladies GAA team as well.'

A small, but important step, in an amazing journey in his ambition to field a Spanish GAA team in the All-Ireland Club Championship.

CURE YOURSELF ... AND KEEP RATS AWAY
ULSTER'S HEALING WELLS CAN DO THE LOT!

Around Ireland there are about 3,000 holy or healing stones and wells which largely predate Christianity from Druid times though the sites are mostly now called after Saints. Some are overtly Christian, such as. St Brigid's Well at Liscannor, which has a huge number of Catholic objects left there by visitors seeking cures.

Unlike Christian stones or crosses e.g. (Ardboe High Cross in Tyrone) which have carvings telling the Bible story these Druid stones and wells carry only Celtic symbols if any at all.

Three of these looked at are in Tyrone at Donacavey, Altadaven and Aghyaran, with another in Donegal at Disert.

Both Altadaven and Aghyaran stones and wells are recognised Druid healing sites whereas the Donacavey stone, originally thought to be early Christian, is attached to a very old graveyard circa 1600 where a chance find in the 1960s, dated back more than 2,000 years, of baby skeletons in pewter vessels, could indicate it was also a place of sacrifice and burial which predates Christianity.

The common feature of the stones is that there is a water-filled hollow in the top of it which collects rainwater. People with eye trouble anoint their eyes with the accumulated water for healing. It was said that if you dropped a pin or other metal object in the hollow all your troubles would vanish or if failing to have anything metallic on you, you simply left or tied the most useless item on your person to the stone or nearest tree.

Thread or rags (clooties), usually red, are a popular item to leave behind principally to ensure a safe pregnancy. Usually, the rags are placed there by people who believe that if a piece of clothing from someone who is ill, pregnant or has a problem of any kind, is hung from the tree, the problem or illness will disappear as the rag rots away.

The use of red thread or cloth is not solely an Irish Christian custom, the significance of the colour red occurs across most major religions because it represents blood and and used with healing pure water, life itself.

The Donacavey, Altadaven and Aghyaran sites all share the same healing properties of remedying sore eyes, warts and other skin problems.

Altadaven is unusual in that it has two sites: St. Brigid's Well, which offers these cures and St. Patrick's Chair. which answers wishes! If you sit on St. Patrick's Chair and make a wish, which you must not tell anyone about, it will be granted within a year.

The Donegal site has the widest range of cures and remedies in Ulster at St. Colmcille's well at Disert which has important extras to the Tyrone stones. It also sorts out bad backs, creaky limbs etc … you simply rub the affected part of the body against the standing stones there. Bad eyesight? No problem. You simply look through the hole in Colmcille's flat stone from both sides and it's sorted for you.

The final extra offered by this site is to get rid of rats. You pick up a handful of soil from near the standing stones…. *very importantly, it must be in your right hand!* If you mix this with mortar and plaster on to walls, it keeps rats away from your house.

Do these remedies actually work? In Druid times, people didn't live very long but in the absence of any other belief, such as Christianity, they probably had a deeper faith in the healing power of the sites and made themselves better through auto-suggestion; a form of personal hypnosis. Other thoughts on them is that the water in the hollow of the stones was rainwater and thus purer than that from a well contaminated by farm animals so rubbing it on your eyes or skin would have a beneficial effect.

One interesting point about the Donacavey and Disert sites is that although they are about 50 miles apart, they are both built on ground containing uranium and in respect of the Disert site, the soil would contain traces of it which would explain the rats remedy: rats avoid uranium.
Coincidence? Or did the Druids know something about natural cures and remedies that has been lost in the mists of time and Christianity?

FAISAL FORTY COATS
The little Libyan man looked up.
at stern faced rugged Irish giants
in short sleeves or vests on a
balmy late September evening

and shivered at the sight.

Mounds of seed spuds bagged up
weighed and marked, Ulster Banners,
British Queens, Kerrs' Pinks, Golden
Wonders,
earlies and mains with 3 or 4 yields yearly
with which he fed the Middle East.

Bargains struck, cash changed hands,
rough sacks piled high on lorries.
'Derry port tomorrow, Scotland next week.
You'll need an extra *geansai[1]*', the driver
laughed.
as Faisal flinched again.

Wondering how such giants survived
this cold windy land and this was early.
mild El 7 areef[2]! How much worse must
El sheta[3] be? Firmly buttoning up his coats
he shuddered at the thought.

Hot whiskies later in the pub in Georges Street
warmed memories of Libya, Cyprus, Greece
and islands where he sold the spuds of Ulster.
and West Scotland. Another great year ahead
and he smiled at the prospect.

Footnote: 1 geansai: Ulster-Scots term for a "thick woollen sweater"; 2:
autumn; 3: winter

THANK YOU FOR TRAVELLING WITH B.E.A[1] TODAY

Passengers on flights to Belfast get you every time, it's the 'characters' you see queueing up at the check in or rushing like madmen to the gate as it is closing, shouting, 'Houl on there to yer hoult!'[2] Yes, as you've probably guessed, it's Ulster Scots meaning 'Hang on there for feck's sake!

All El Al flights have at least one armed Mossad security person on board, probably more, flights to Belfast have at least three 'characters'. They have not varied much over time and are the bloke with a bad haircut (usually coloured stripes), another wearing a leather Cowboy hat and/or New Zealand Shepherd's waterproof long coat with the third proudly wearing an autographed Celtic shirt, who frequently doubles up as the bad haircut bloke.

On this BEA flight from Birmingham in December 1966 we also had two celebrities, a well-known TV soap star and the most gifted Northern Irish footballer, pre-George Best, largely unknown in England, having mainly played on the continent who when 17 years old was getting rave notices in the Irish League and sports pages as 'Ireland's Jimmy Greaves'... then later headlines across the world.[3]

---

[1] BEA (British European Airways) was an earlier brand name before British Airways

[2] https://www.bbc.co.uk/northernireland/voices/atilazed/h.shtml
[The 'Des' contributor here is not me.]

[3]

https://www.theguardian.com/sport/blog/2011/nov/02/forgott en-story-john-crossan-ban Johnny Crossan the most harshly treated footballer of all time

You hoped to avoid the 'characters' and I did…all three of them were seated together. I was lucky to get a seat next to the footballer who caught the eye in his sharp Italian suit, great haircut and physique with first class treatment from the air hostess since he spoke in French as she leaned closely over him to check his seatbelt was fastened.

'Ah, oui', c'est parti!' (Yes, let's go!')

He smiled as he said to me, 'You get far better service on here pretending to be French!'[4]

'A good result today', I said.

He nodded, 'Yes, Tony Brown and Jeff Astle are difficult to handle but we managed it. So who do you follow in Birmingham?'

'West Brom and Villa, especially Villa because of Peter McParland and Derek Dougan in the past .'

'Both great players for NI, I'd hate to be a goalie tackling Peter… Derek 'Apache' is a terrific laugh! Fancy a drink?'

He waved at the air hostess. who was immediately there, 'Deux whiskies sur glace, s'il vous plait.'

---

[4] https://www.manchestereveningnews.co.uk/sport/football/football-news/my-guardian-angel---johnny-crossan-852918 Paul 'Scoop' Hince

'Do you remember Peter Doherty? [5]My mentor and inspiration. I'm just popping over to see him.'

'Yes of course, everybody remembers Peter, we got time off school for the NI games in 1958.'
We chatted about both football and GAA.
As the descent into Aldergrove started, there was a bit of a commotion at the front with the soap star refusing to sit down and demanding another drink, until pushed down and buckled in by the crew.

When we finally rolled to a halt, she staggered up, swaying slightly in the aisle, refusing to leave as she was expecting to be met by Arts Promoters for photos outside the plane but there was no red carpet nor promoters in sight.

Finally, the hostess called the ground staff and a burly bloke in fluorescent orange wear came up the steps to confront her.

'WHO ARE YOU??? DO YOU KNOW WHO AND WHAT I AM???'

'Course I do. I'm Bob from Ballymena, thanks for asking by the way. You're Meg Richardson[6] from Crossroads, and

---

[5] https://www.nationalfootballmuseum.com/halloffame/peter-doherty/

Peter Doherty captained Manchester City and was top scorer when they won the First Division title. Better known as an inspirational Manager taking Northern Ireland to the World Cup Quarter Finals in 1958, the smallest squad of professional players and smallest Football Association ever to reach the QFs.
[6] British Newspapers Archive Belfast Telegraph Thursday 15th December 1966 FESTIVAL OF CAROLS Belfast on Sunday Guests

you're pissed, totally stocious!!!', bending down to grab her around the legs and throw her over his shoulder in a fireman's lift saying,

'Ye want to avoid that Scottish stuff on the plane, it's cheap rubbish. Black Bush for me every time. Ye simply can't beat a wee Black & White on ice to say cheerio to work at the end of the shift, keeps my cousins employed at Bushmills as well, as a bonus', as he carried her down the steps to the waiting electric buggy, strapped her in and headed to Arrivals. Both air hostesses sighed with relief to finally see the back of her.

'Ye must meet some strange people in your line of business,' said the 'character' in the leather cowboy hat and New Zealand shepherd coat as he passed them.

'Ye're bang on there,' agreed both the bad haircut and autographed Celtic blokes following him.

'Ay couldn't be doing dealing with mad people all the time,' added the bad haircut one.

They all nodded in agreement with each other.

Both crew members managed to keep a straight face simply replying, 'Thank you for travelling with BEA today.'

Walking up from baggage retrieval past the Lagan Bar, I noticed Meg was being propped upright in her chair by two Belfast Arts people, one in a cravat, the other in a bow tie.

---

will be UTV announcer Mike Lovell Meg Richardson of television's Crossroads programme, Noele Gordon. Also taking part in the service will be the Ulster Girls' Choir, the Victoria Male Voice Choir and Macrory Memorial.

She had clearly taken Bob's advice, with a bottle of Black Bush already about half empty on the table, as she gazed through the window wondering,

'Who is that man, who is he?', as the footballer posed for photos and signed autographs outside.

Johnny Crossan had followed his mentor Peter Doherty as captain of Manchester City but his City career ended after a bad car crash. He later returned to Derry to set up and run sport shops and pubs. He still played football locally, 3 days a week, up to his 70s. Now aged 80 he commentates and does football analysis for BBC Radio Foyle.

Footnote: Football fans may appreciate the following:

NI QF 1958 Team Only one member is still alive: Peter McParland (Aston Villa).

Derek Dougan was a controversial figure who Chaired the PFA for 7 years ceaselessly pursuing footballers' rights, became Chairman of Wolves, TV pundit and writer (On the Spot, Attack, The Sash He Never Wore, How Not to Run Football, Book of Soccer, The Footballer (Novel)) who fielded the first All Ireland Team (since 1949) in 1973 but was refused permission by both the IFA/FAI to use Ireland as its name. The team played as Shamrock Rovers XI against Brazil in Dublin in 1973 and were beaten 4-3. (The first time in 8 years that Brazil had conceded 3 goals).

Harry Gregg https://www.irishtimes.com/sport/soccer/english-soccer/bravery-and-goodness-harry-gregg-the-reluctant-hero-of-munich-1.3378025 the most expensive Goal keeper in the World in 1957, voted Best Goalkeeper, World Cup 1958 had similar views on Irish National teams   'I am delighted they are doing well again and for the people who watch,' he said, 'but I will be frank. I was lucky enough to play in a team of players born and bred in Ireland. To me that's very important.'

'I don't want to hurt people but the team I played in were Irish. Good luck to those in the team now. They have my support.' (Daily Mail 13th October 2017)

Jeff Astle Deceased 2002. Believed to be caused by s brain damage ustained from heading heavy leather footballs.

Tony Brown. Oldham born, discovered while playing for Manchester Boys Football Team.

Author's note: My own interests are largely in comedy and/or unusual happenings from the past and I hope that this comes through with a smile on both.

The group comprises wide variety of writers, poets and playwrights who can help or offer advice on what you write.

Having a variety of colleagues who have had work published, self-published or acted out on stage is very helpful for someone starting out who can draw on their experience for their own projects. Long may it continue.

KATHLEEN HANDRICK

Kathleen was born and lives in Oldham. Her father came from County Mayo and her mother from Lancashire. She has welcomed the opportunity to explore her Irish heritage through shared writing and research.

Kathleen joined Manchester Irish Writers in 2013, just prior to the publication of the *Changing Skies* anthology. As a novice writer she found the challenge of writing quite daunting but was encouraged by the feedback and help from the group. This has continued over the years.

She finds that the writers' group gives the opportunity to experience and learn from the variety and standard of work produced by the writers. She especially enjoys the evenings when the group share their work with a wider audience. The last few years have been difficult to organise but Zoom 'meetings' have enabled the companionship and sharing of ideas to continue and has provided humour for her writing too.

STIRABOUT

1930s. A small court. Pat (late 30s) walks out of a house and sits on a chair at the door. He is dressed in a working shirt and waistcoat and removes a watch from his pocket to check the time. He returns the watch and places his hands on his thighs.

Pull up that stool there and rest yourself for a few minutes. It's a grand evening so I'm having a breather out here before I take the children out. The stirabout's on the stove– Molly's watching it. She's a great girl but ...she can be stubborn ... just like her mother!

Her mother? Ah, she was a farmer's daughter and me... I was a labourer's son. So there was no fortune there – I can tell you! You see her father had plans for her to wed a neighbour for the land and sure when he heard about me *and* the child -well we had to get away from Wexford quickly, you know what I mean. So with a bit o' money from her sister and our own few shillings we scraped the fare to England.

That was a rough journey for sure. 'I thought my father would have been different – helped us.' Sarah just kept sobbing - how he'd always loved her, and he was kind-hearted and so on. I was helpless. I couldn't say what I was thinking - that he didn't show much kindness when he found out about us. I just stayed quiet and tried to comfort her as best I could but … I don't know women's ways.

I knew of some fellas from New Ross who were working in the cotton mills here in Oldham and I had the mind to do the same. Have you heard the 'clack-clack-clack' of those looms, though … the heat…the dust sticking in your mouth! It wasn't for me... from the fields and the river. Anyway, thanks be to God, the railway needed plate layers. I got myself taken on; I'm in the open; I can breathe easier, and it suits me fine.

We'd only been here a few months when Molly was born. The sadness was still on Sarah, missing her family, but she wouldn't let on and now she had the wee girl to cheer her. I'd say we settle down a bit as a family then. I was out working hard to keep us; Sarah was busy with the child and we rolled along.

A year or so on and there was another one on the way and at last she said, 'Pat I think you're right; we *should* be married. I know now there will be no blessing from my father. I might as well be dead to him and it's not fair to keep you hanging on. You're all that matters to me now.'

I'd been after her to get married, you see, ever since we came to England. Of course, I knew that living in sin was wrong and listen here, the flames of hell seemed a far better prospect than going up to that Chapel to explain ourselves to Father Walsh. He gave out to us alright– wagging his finger. 'You'll have to be quick then, so you will! I don't want a marriage *and* a baptism on the same day!' Thank God, though, he went easy on us and gave us his blessing.
You know, this little Court, it's home to folk from all over – Dublin, Clare, Mayo – not forgetting Wexford of course! Well, that night was great, I tell you! We had songs, stories, a few sets and a drop or two. Sarah was like a girl again. It did my heart good to see her. Great neighbours is what you need. There's no secrets or peace though – everyone's on top of each other - laughing, shouting, arguing... children running around barefoot, playing with any old sticks and stones. You'll even get a good song from that line of privvies of an evening after work!

Well, by and by, our little family grew. We had Molly and Tom and then Bridgie arrived. That was a struggle- another mouth to feed. We all help each other out though. We need to – in hard times. I'd sit Tom up on a chair in the yard and cut his hair with some shears I'd brought from home. Then it'd start ... 'Pat, will you just tidy Owen up for me while you're there', or 'When you've the time, Pat, can I send Daniel over...' Loads o' that kind! You could say now, I'm the barber for all the lads here... and beyond, with me shears!

Anyway - Sarah was busy with the youngsters and thanks be to God, she seemed easier in her mind. But when she'd get those letters from her sister, I tell you, she'd read them; set her face; fold them and crease them and tuck them in her pocket –all without a word. She wouldn't bend a bit!

'Why don't you write to your father?' I said it the once but believe me...I hadn't the courage to say it again. It destroyed her. To deny his own a bit o' happiness like that. What does it matter who you are or where you come from? I tell you I'm an honest, working man and I can raise my family without the likes of him or his money. God help us though, we could ha' done with a bit extra at times, especially when wee Annie came along.

Annie wasn't two years old - Sarah was patching some sheets and pricked her finger on the needle. She took a fever the next day and then a couple o' days later, she was gone. Biddy brought new sheets over, so Sarah wouldn't have to be laid out on patched ones in the room back there. It was a kindly thing to do. I got a message from her sister. She was sorry for my troubles – that it ended this way. She knew I'd done my best and Sarah had been happy with me and the family. She didn't mention the father.

I was lost there for a while, I tell you. Four young children – what was a man to do. I couldn't go back home that's for sure. Thanks be to God for these neighbours, though. With their help, I've raised them on my own. 'Aah - what's a couple extra when I have a brood of my own to feed! Get yourself off to work Pat.'

I'd 'a never managed myself, I know. Oh yes, I've had offers from one or two widows – good women -and some not so good, if it be known. But Sarah was the only one for me, that's for sure. We manage alright. I save a few pennies a week for Wednesday – the kids love it...the variety shows or the picture house. That's why we have the stirabout for tea. There's no money left for a bit o' meat or potatoes.

Ach – speaking o' stirabout, it'll be ready now. I'd better dish it up quick or I'll have the four o' them giving out at me for a week if we miss the show and I can't be doing with that!

Author's note: I wrote 'Stirabout' for the Manchester Irish Writers when I joined in 2013. It was a monologue for the proposed Changing Skies *anthology and production. It was a daunting experience for a new writer, but I received much encouragement from the other writers which has continued over the years. I have edited the monologue since then but chose to include it as it is based on a family story and was my first endeavour at writing.*

THE UNION OF THE FIELDS

The lingering scent of turf didn't quite mask the musty smell of the lifeless cottage, but Lizzie breathed in contentedly as she stood in the doorway. She usually only visited on Saturdays, to light the fire, relax in her mother's chair and think. She wished sometimes that she could stop thinking but it was too late for that now.

It was only two days ago since she was here but this evening was Hallowe'en, the eve of All Saints' Day, *'Oiche Shamhna'*. Lizzie had come to the cottage to pray for her parents and she would do this for the next two evenings when she had finished her chores above at the house. The fire was already laid, she just had to take a taper and light it. She smoothed the faded cushions on the two fireside chairs, straightened the antimacassars, lovingly embroidered by her mother so long ago, and went to sit on the settle by the hearth. She wouldn't use her mother's chair this evening. Lizzie closed her eyes.

Was it only two years ago? What a foolish woman, what silly notions; why, oh why, did I do it?

That, too, was All Hallows' Eve. Lizzie had straightened her parents' photographs on the dresser, placed a lighted candle on the windowsill and sat to pray for their souls. Three years had passed since they had died, within six weeks of each other, and she missed them. She had considered leaving food out for them, and pulling their chairs away from the dining table so they could sit if they visited, but told herself that was the old ways, not now. She recalled those traditions of her mother and the apple bobbing and bonfires with the neighbours; the carefree life she had once led. Now, though, she was a woman nearing forty, living alone.

What on earth was I thinking of? I suppose I was remembering that eighteen-year-old Lizzie, full of romantic notions.

Lizzie recalled how it happened. She had taken a sharp knife and an apple and cut the peel without breaking it, just as she had as a young girl. She had thrown it over her shoulder but this time she could see the S-shape on the floor. A thrill of excitement, or was it fear, ran through her before she chided herself. You're a grown woman. Stop. It can't be. You have no feelings for him.

She concluded her whispered prayers and stood to cross to the table. As she did, she caught sight of herself in the mirror opposite. For a fleeting moment, there was another figure too- that greying thatch of hair, undeniably Sean. The teenage Lizzie had seen nothing when she had done this back then but now, she was sure she had seen the vision. Stop. It's just the shape of the apple skin she told herself. Stop being foolish. You are a grown woman.

Lizzie didn't call it pestering but there was persistence in Sean. He had suggested it several times since her parents ' death. She had a couple of fields, he had a few more, sure wouldn't it make sense to join them together. But that is not how a marriage should be, she told herself each time.

The Hallowe'en happenings stayed with her though and as Christmas drew near and Sean suggested that they eat together, she accepted. She declined his invitation to cook at his house, that would not be right, but instead she provided a small feast for them to share. He had given her a pretty, lacy scarf. 'It was my mother's', he muttered awkwardly, as he left it on the table. Lizzie was not offended by this but touched by his kind thought. Altogether, she had found the day's experience rather pleasant as he sat opposite her in her father's chair, smoking his pipe in the silence.

A few weeks later, Sean had brought up the joining of the fields again. Did she not think it made sense? She was not a young woman anymore, he pointed out and he wasn't getting any younger either. He was, she thought, fifteen years older than her so they were not exactly equals. This time, however, she had mellowed. Perhaps it was the thought of that Christmas evening or even that Hallowe'en sighting. I don't believe in all that really but perhaps it was a sign.

The settle wasn't as comfortable as her mother's chair, and she stretched, opened her eyes and looked around the room.

Look at me now. Eighteen months married. Eighteen months since the union of the fields. Sean's not a bad husband, is he? Hmm, I'm not really able to judge. He's the only husband I have known. Should there be more though? He has my fields, what do I have? He provides for me; I keep house for him; we work together in our fields. He lets me keep my cottage here to visit and I can enjoy these few hours in the stillness before I go back to him- sitting by the fire in his silence. Two years ago, I was alone and now I have Sean. That's the way it is now and perhaps it was meant to be.

Author's note: I wrote The Union of the Fields *as a Hallowe'en story, but it developed into an exploration of women's choices in rural Ireland in the past. It was prompted by a revelation of an arranged marriage in the 1950s in Mayo. Lizzie's marriage was not because of a matchmaker of old but from loneliness and a human desire for security and company.*

ANN HEATHCOTE

Ann, a Manchester poet, was ensnared by poetry in 2015 and has been writing on a serious basis ever since. Her poetry reflects her previous career as a psychotherapist and her experiences as a second-generation Irish immigrant. Ann joined the Manchester Irish Writers group in May 2017. She finds being a member of the group both invaluable and enjoyable. She particularly appreciates the camaraderie, the incidental learning about Irish history and culture, and most of all the expert feedback she receives on her poetry. Ann has had her poems published in several poetry journals, anthologies and shortlisted in a few poetry competitions.

POEM WITH A POTATO IN IT

I remember the tea table:
boiled potatoes in their skins,
salty ham shanks with cabbage.

So many ways to prepare a potato.
Boiled, fried, mashed, baked.
The Irish way is boiled.

My father threw the little ones away.
The little ones are my favourites—
but my history does not include hunger.

Inspired by Robert Hass & Hannah Lowe

AN IRISH IMMIGRANT MOTHER MESSES WITH HER CHILD'S HEAD

Who's that? At this hour?
Quick take the cups into the kitchen,
hide away the newspaper under the chair,
fluff up the cushions, turn the tele off.
Open the door - don't leave them standing!

Oh, it's yourself, fancy that.
No, no, it's no trouble at all.
Come on in - make yourself at home.
For sure, for sure, it's lovely to see you.
How ya doing? And what about your mother?
Would you like a cup of tea or a whiskey?
A sandwich or a piece of apple pie?
Go on, you must have something,
now I won't take no for an answer.

Fancy them coming at this time,
in the middle of Eamonn Andrews.
They could have called.
Hasn't she put on weight?
Isn't it dreadful,
they've put their mother in a home,
after all she's done for them.

Sure, it will come to us all one day.

THE MOTHER WHO HID THE APPLES

Mother squirrelled away the brown paper bag
filled with red apples

When the time was right (for her)
mother carried the brown paper bag
into the living room with a breakfast bowl
and sharp knife

As mother peeled the apples
we sat at her feet
fighting for apple peel
delighted
if it
all
came
off
in
one
long
strip

MARY ANNE HICKEY TELLS HER STORY OF THE MANCHESTER MARTYRS 1867 – IN 12 UNEQUAL PARTS

My fiancé Will is a hot head,
nineteen.
Like my Da - passionate
about Ireland's freedom.

*   *   *   17th September
Tuesday, Will shakes his foot,
taps his fingers,
tells me nothing.
We kiss a quick goodnight.

*   *   *   18th September
Wednesday, I hear rumours –
two Fenian leaders escape,
the arrest of twenty-five Irish men,
a policeman shot dead.

*   *   *

An anti-Irish mob run riot
through the streets of Manchester.
My Will's beaten and stoned,
arrested, they say, for killing the cop.

*   *   *

I stay in my digs,
lay on my bed,
stare at damp patches
in the corners of the ceiling.

*   *   *   20th September
Friday, the law needs a scapegoat.
Will didn't do it -
I'm as innocent as the child unborn.
I believe him.

*   *   *   28th October
Monday, five men brought to court.
Each witness drilled.
No fairness in this

anti-Fenian fervour.

* * * 1ˢᵗ November
Friday, my Will's sentenced to death:
I am innocent. I'll have no mercy.
I will die proudly in defence of an oppressed
and enslaved people. God save Ireland.

* * * 14ᵗʰ November
Thursday, ten days before the scaffold,
I can visit my Will in prison.
I reach for his hands, hold his face,
stare into his grey eyes and cry.

* * *

Will prays for a reprieve -
swings between hope and despair.
If God can't save Ireland,
how can he save Will.

* * * 22ⁿᵈ November
Friday, the day before the gallows -
I'm turned away
from the prison gates.
Clouds hang heavy - turn inky grey.

* * * 23ʳᵈ November
Today, the noose breaks his neck -
I thank God his death is swift.
No marriage, no sweetheart,
no more my Will.

Inspired by Joseph O'Neill (2012). The Manchester
Martyrs, *Cork: Mercier Press.*

63

THE IRISH IN ENGLAND –
IN THE WORDS OF FRIEDRICH
ENGELS 1845

*(A found poem from the chapter on Irish
Immigration by Friedrich Engels in* Condition
of the Working Class in England, *1845)*

The Irish …
enter great cities
insinuate themselves everywhere
rough, intemperate, improvident
grown without civilization
from the lowest class
more strength than skill—
bricklayers, porters, jobbers
require less wages
degrade the English workingmen
bring all their brutal habits
build pigsties against their houses
love their pigs as the Arab their horses
deposit garbage and filth before their doors
poison the air
eat potatoes, potatoes, potatoes
clothes held together by a single thread
unaccustomed to furniture—
piece of wood, broken chair, old chest for a
table
heap of straw, a few rags for a bed
chairs, doorposts, flooring, find their way up
the chimney
revel in bestial drunkenness
singing, aspirate brogue
dissolute, unsteady, on too low a plane

crudity places them near level with the savage
poor devils, society shuts them out

WHEN ARTIO CALLS YOUR NAME

Goddess of the Celts, protector of young—Artio.
She-bear. Silver-tipped hair shimmers
in the light of the Lammas moon.

Seven foot high, four hundred pounds, one blow
of her paw will floor you. Safe guardian
of wild animals. Dream keeper.

At home in mountains, thick forests. Forages
in spring and summer. Basks in the sun.
When the first shivers of autumn ruffle her brown
fur,

she eats in readiness for her winter's toil.
As snow coats northern slopes, she digs
a den deep in the frozen earth.

There she gives birth, suckles her young,
buffers them from cold—until melting snow
signals spring.
When you yearn for a mother   hush   listen

Artio is calling your name.

Inspired by Artio, Celtic Goddess of Wildlife,
Transformation and Abundance, *by Judith Shaw on 26
August 2015, on feminismandreligion.com*

*Author's note: When I 'dared' approach the Manchester
Irish Writers group in 2017, I was unsure if I was eligible*

65

to join. Even though I have only Irish blood and an Irish heart, as a second-generation Irish immigrant I sound English. I need not have worried. The group welcomed me with open arms. The poems I have shared here were all written during my time in the Manchester Irish Writers group and reflect the breadth of the topics we cover from the mythical to the political and everything in between.

ALRENE HUGHES

Alrene was born in Enniskillen, grew up in Belfast, then moved to Manchester. She co-founded the Manchester Irish Writers with Rose Morris in 1994. For a long while she wrote poetry and short stories. Then in 2014 she left the group to write novels: *Martha's Girls, The Golden Sisters, A Song in My Heart, The Girl in the Pink Raincoat,* and *The Girl from the Corner Shop.*

ESTABLISHING TEMPO

It arrives
Unaccompanied by memories
A thin square box,
green leather, green satin.
A medal
not a soldier's … a soprano's.
My fingers trace a harp
And 'Feis Ceoil 1906'.

On the journey south
she studies her music,
pitches each note in her head
hears the accompaniment begin,
establish tempo …
No border. Only stewed tea
and cake at Dundalk.
A gradual shift from
northern nasal vowels
to soft southern consonants.

In the afternoon she walks
the length of O'Connell Street
in a hobble skirt and wide brimmed hat,

buys stamps at the GPO,
practises her breathing in Phoenix Park.
Mouths, sounds phonetically perfect.

Early evening, in a glow of gas light,
she steps on stage, opening bars play
and the girl from the north sings
in Irish …

I hold her medal in my hand.
Establish tempo.

DONAGHADEE

I know now why he liked it.
An unremarkable dot on the coast,
squat cottages huddled round
the harbour, which curved,
finger-like into the Irish Sea,
beckoning his native Scotland.
At its tip, a lighthouse
Stark and striking.

Donaghadee: worth the effort
To shape each syllable.
Worth the six miles from Bangor,
'For the fresh air,' he said.
Always the same, a dander
stopping to the look down at
the little boats bobbing below,
tarry ropes chaffing the capstan.

On to which he would swing me,
so I could be as tall as him.
And always the wind, salty sharp.

He filled his lungs like an addict,
the Senior Service pocketed.
From the broad sea wall
He'd point out the Copelands,
island of angry birds.

On the edge of the open sea,
wee boys perched fussing
over half-crown fishing lines.
'Did ye catch anything?'
'Aye Mister. D'ye wanna see?
Flash of silver in a bucket.
He straightened up, breathed deeply.
I know now why he liked it.

MANCHESTER SKIES

Early morning
The boat train rattles into Exchange Station.
Outside, gun-metal clouds
Lie low over blackened buildings.
Fine drizzle coats our clothes, faces, hair.

Midday
Miles Platting, straight off the street, two up
two down.
A stiff breeze reveals snatches a pale sky.

Shafts of sunlight illuminate
Years of dirt and grime.

Afternoon
Pans of scalding water, carbolic fumes
We scrub paintwork, windows, floors.
Net curtains flap on the line beneath

A tiny blue rectangle stretched over the yard.

Midnight
Half-light, a city sky
Devoid of darkness, moon and stars
Only the eerie glow of orange street lights
And the sweeping beams of cars.

Morning
We ride a bus to the end of the line
In search of the horizon
And find our sky – complete, huge,
welcoming.
We fill our lungs with sweet clean air
And let our sore hearts – soar.

SODA BREAD

Visiting relatives brought presents
Floury farls of soda bread
Twisted in tissue paper
A taste of home.

We'd devour them
Hungry for comfort.
Knowing they wouldn't keep.
Left a day
They'd turn green
Tainted in the English air.
There's soda bread in Tesco's now.
I never buy it.

SUZANNE JEANS

Suzanne was born and brought up on the Wirral. She taught Drama and Theatre Studies for over 30 years in the north-west of England before taking early retirement in 2017. Suzanne joined the Manchester Irish Writers in early 2018. She decided to put pen to paper and has since written a play and three short stories. Her first short story – *Whiteout* – was chosen for publication in a short story anthology in January 2019.

In October 2019, Suzanne won the Kenneth Branagh International New Drama Writing Award at the Windsor Fringe Festival, for her semi-autobiographical one act play, *An Absence Of.* The play was then developed, extended and performed as a workshop production at the *Actors & Writers London* play-reading forum in 2021.

In 2023 Suzanne wrote a short story, *The Soft Rope*, inspired by the writing of James Joyce. It was subsequently longlisted for the Bridport Short Story Competition and the Bath Short Story Award. It was also shortlisted for the Wells Festival of Literature Short Story Award. A second story – *The Cut* – inspired by the Magdalene laundries scandal, has recently been submitted to a number of competitions.

Suzanne lives in Littleborough where she looks after her two grandsons, potters in the garden, and tries in vain to keep fit. When time and inspiration allow, she still writes and lives in hope that one day, she may be able to return to her play *An Absence Of* to develop it for production.

THE SILENCE OF SNOW

One

It is the absence of sound that brings her back. The rain has stopped and the silence returns her to the now.

The first thing she sees when she opens her eyes is the swing hanging. The twisted chain, red plastic seat indolent, neck-broken, shining then shadowed in the amber glare of the security light.

Shining. Shadowed.

She looks around. Black dirt under nails. She clenches her fingers, tightening them into an unconvincing fist, and the mud reluctantly oozes. Hair drenched, drips escape, run to her chin, congregate, then with a slight shake of her head, drop, briefly caught in the light then gone. Shine. Shadow. She stays motionless until the security light snaps off with a dull click. More attentive now, the urge comes from nowhere, to shake herself like a dog. She stretches out a hand. Mud and clay are beginning to coagulate, congealing between her bruised fingers.

She is naked. She is sitting in the middle of the lawn. This realization brings no astonishment, no alarm.

The darkness is total. She inhales deeply but her chest hurts. Turning slightly, the smallest of intimations, and this time the light blinds her, immobilizing her but not before she has seen the stark outline of the spade leaning against the wall.

Sluggish, she waits for the pain deep inside her chest to lessen. No rush. Breathe and wait. Breathe. Wait. And the rain comes again. No gentle drizzle this as it slices, slashing ice through the air. From over the hill towards town, a solitary firework explodes into life, showering the night sky with dazzling, dancing red droplets. Blood stars.

The atmosphere around her is stagnant with waiting. The sheer effort of rising, of making a start, uncrossing her stiffened legs, is beyond her now. A soft moan. Exhaling, her limbs limp and loosening, she slips onto her side. She caresses the pillow of soil with her fingertips, then her cheek. Her lips kiss the cold, wet earth.

She longs for sleep.

Eyes closed now she feels the rain pooling in the creases of her elbows, knees, collecting in her unprotected, upturned palms. Her little finger twitches, beckoning. High above her, what has been sleet becomes fuller, thicker, gentler. Flakes dance and fall. Her open palm receives the gift of white soft down, and as the temperature drops further, her frozen form settles, cushioned and comfortable.

It is a while before the snowfall swathes her completely with a quilted coat of ice, concealing the mud, the leaves, the detritus of what lies hidden. By morning, as the sun rises reluctantly, the sky a grim grey shroud, she is covered in a snow shawl and at first glance all that can be seen is a hardened hand, blue fingers like brittle chicken bones.

Two

Roy whistles tunelessly as he waits for the kettle to boil. Pinching a teabag between his stained fingers, he drops it into his favourite mug. As steam fills the kitchen he leans on the edge of the sink, narrows his eyes and gazes out into the garden, whose form is obscured by the heavy snowfall.

He reaches instinctively behind him for the switch as his mind drifts over what lies beneath the snow. Bulbs and tubers hidden in the dark, waiting for Spring to awaken. Despite the warmth in the kitchen, he shivers. A ghost walking over his grave.

His mind is still elsewhere as he adds a generous heap of sugar and the tiniest splash of milk. For the briefest of moments, he smiles sheepishly and remembers Joan teasing him about the industrial strength of his brew throughout the duration of their very contented marriage.

He misses her.

Not given to excessive sentiment, and not wishing to spoil this first day of the New Year, Roy shrugs off his momentary melancholia and pulls a thick fleece over his head, trying to avoid the zip snagging on his abundant beard. He reaches for his gardening gloves with one hand and his tea with the other and busies himself prioritizing the list of jobs he has lined up for completion before the daylight fades and the temperature plunges again.

On the doorstep the first breath he takes is tentative. It is bitterly cold. A perfect day. He has spent the last few years, since retirement, since Joan passed on, working on their large garden and allotment. He knows soil. Knows plants. How they behave, how they respond, how they need to be teased or tormented into life. It's a few years now since the temperature has dropped so low overnight and for a brief moment he is lulled by the temperateness and comfort of his kitchen, the flabby fireside chair, the hypnotic hush of the radio. Resigned to the necessity of feeling useful, to know that the day is not wasted regardless of the arctic blast, he pulls on his boots, thrusts his hands deep into the gloves and stomps his way through the drifts towards the greenhouse.

Snug inside, he busies himself potting up seedlings, instinctively, effortlessly at peace. The routine is almost ritualistic in its repetition, demanding both patience and a lightness of touch. Qualities Roy has in spades. A flicker outside catches his eye and he looks up. A red breasted robin sits on the fence post, snow almost concealing its fluffy belly, bright, beady eyes darting. Roy whistles in appreciation and the robin inclines its head in response. Joan loved the birds visiting their garden, especially towards the end. Roy smiles.

Roy is comfortable and contented as the morning becomes afternoon. If not for the sudden rumbling of his stomach, he would have remained there until the sun began to slip down behind the conifer hedge, in blissful ignorance of all that was to come. But as his tummy gently growls with the first pangs of hunger, he remembers.

Annie.

He has promised Annie he will deliver winter spinach over the New Year period. Intending to drop by the previous day, he had got caught up in the nostalgia and reminiscences of the last day of the year, wallowing self-indulgently with beer, then brandy, towards the midnight tolling of Big Ben. He would drop over to see her shortly. It was only a 20-minute walk. Maybe longer given the snow drifts, but it would be a satisfying end to his day.

He doesn't want to admit that he has a soft spot for Annie. Joan teased him mercilessly about it over the years, though always with a sense of humour about the absurdity of his misplaced affections. Yes, he'd go to see Annie. See if she wanted anything else. He could always fix the trellis that had fallen during the storm last week. With luck, she might have been baking and the offer of tea and scones in front of the fire might be forthcoming. Roy digs his hands into the soft, crumbly compost and chuckles softly to himself.

Three

If she. One more. One. Last night. Bitter chatter choke.
She. Coming.
Clack. Clack. Red heels.   Oak high shine of wood.
Gleaming. Ridiculous pointy, red, weapon-heeled shoes.
Clack. Click. Clack.
My floor. Take your bloody shoes off.
Buzzing is back. Started again. Clack. Chat. Choke.
Robin on the swing. Robin red seat. Fix it, twisting neck there. Ask Roy next time. Soft spot.
Clack. Clack click . Grit teeth. Jaw. Clenching. Clenching. Hurting.
Starts again. She. Moan, mocking, whinge, whine. Whine and now white. Buzzing. Buzzing white. Fit to burst. Buzz white pain. Red hot. Hurting.
Need out. To get. Out. Air.
-   *Bloody freezing out there. You must be mad.*
Clack. Clack. Stabbing red hot heels.
-   *Snow forecast. Bloody typical. Won't get a taxi all the way up here now.*
Go before heels click clack red
Out. Robin gone. Sharp air. Shrill. Cuts through. Buzzing and clacking and white.
Cold. Silence. Clack gone. Buzz gone. Silent.
    No click
        clack
            pointy red stab.

76

Four

Roy approaches Annie's house with a slight tremor in his gloved hands and a spring in his step, which given the treacherous conditions underfoot is bordering on reckless. If asked, he would put the tremor down to a surfeit of caffeine and dismiss the fanciful idea that he might be anticipating seeing Annie rather more than is seemly in a man three years short of his 70th birthday.

The curtains are drawn. Unusual but nothing to be alarmed about. He recalls in the same instant, Annie telling him that Sophie is visiting over Christmas and New Year. Annie is discreet - secretive Joan used to say - and the impression he has formed over the years is that mother and daughter have a difficult relationship. "Tricky' is the only word he remembers Annie ever using about her daughter. "Things are… tricky… with Sophie," she had confessed over coffee on the only occasion to date that he had been invited into the house. Her face had been set in an expression of grim resignation that Roy recognized ruefully from over 30 years of marriage to Joan. He had known better than to delve deeper. Instead, he had nodded, his mouth full of coffee and walnut cake.

Now he treads with care up the incline of the drive, the snowdrifts past his knees. As he rounds the corner. he is momentarily blinded by the glare of the late afternoon sun on the sweep of lawn, and the magnificence of the vista that lies before him. Annie's property is one of the finest in the village with formal landscaped gardens stretching all the way down to the river. The unbroken, unblemished snow dazzles with radiance. Roy narrows his eyes against the brilliance and trudges over to the back door, his lumbering boots scarring the flawless snow. He raises his gloved hand to knock.

The door is ajar. Snow, blown in by the fierce wind, lies like a gentle blanket folded casually against the skirting. He feels the first tickle of unease but only acknowledges this later.

After.

His eyes return to the landscape, to what was familiar now made strange. The path is barely distinguishable as it winds its way down past Sophie's old swing, red seat askew, towards the willow grove and river beyond. A robin sits on top of the swing. It watches Roy and with jaunty economy of movement, hops away and alights on the handle of a spade, partially submerged, lying sprawled alongside the shed.

Five

Shed. Silent. Smells.
Earthy. Musty. Comfort of compost. Tools. Regimented. Suspended. Hoes. Spades. Cutting and pruning and potting and snipping and delving and digging and burying.
Not long now. Snow. Sky full, tip top.
Robin back. Beady eye.
Prickle.
And she's coming.
She's watching.
Breathe. Snow but not yet. Not now. Buzzzzz. Need to stop. White hurting, red hot.
Take spade. Outside. Blast of cold. Out to the middle. Dig. Yes. Keep red away. Yes, spade. Comfort. Yes.
Gripping, turning, twisting, pushing. The buzz pain white. She's here.
Sweating and panting and digging and shoveling. Clack clack clop of the red stabbing heels. Prickle and rigid my head pain and she. Mocking, moaning, whine

- *You're mad, you are, mad!*
Sharp face bitter lip, nasty. Spits, stabs, dragging down to
pain to buzz white deeper where I can't
- *Christ I hate you .Going now, can't stand another
minute*
Digging and digging, bury the buzz pain, breathe deeper
down the white
- *Hate you. Mad witch.*
Pointy shoes. Stupid pointy shoes, red soles, red heels. Mud
and soil and leaves and clay.
She. Laughing.
- *Mad witch!*
Loud buzz pain everywhere around me, inside, can't see.
Can't hear, pain white buzz buzz and she grabs
grabs
spade
and she.
I push
we
push and
buzz, bite down hard and hard again and   a g a i n
bloody lips jaws clench and again again again and
W H I T E.

Six
Roy hesitates, his hand on the door frame. Maybe he'd be
better off trying the front door, the bell. But he knows from
years of helping Annie tend the garden, she barely uses the
front, preferring the back and route through the garden. He
removes a glove and knocks on the window. His knuckles,
liberated from their warm cocoon, tingle with the cold. He
waits.

Roy chews his lip, frowns deeply, turns and glances once
more over the frozen terrain, searching for anything

79

resembling footprints not his own. Unlikely she'd be out in this anyway, so where? He racks his brain to recall their last conversation, her plans for over the holiday. Did she say she was going away? He doesn't think so. No, Sophie is... the open door....

He stamps decisively to knock the snow from his boots. For appearances sake he calls her name before stepping inside, but his voice echoes, is swallowed and gone. On the table a half-eaten sandwich, knife edged with solidified butter. Two cups of unfinished coffee.

Under his layers of wool and fleece, the tickle becomes an itch.

He is nervous about going further in this house. Nearly 20 years he has been coming here and not once has he set foot beyond the kitchen. He is surprised to find that his heart rate has increased, though not unpleasantly so. He is also embarrassed to discover that being alone in Annie's house, in her territory, is, in some primal way, thrilling to him. This is not a confession he will later share with the police.

Seven

Annie knows. Once she gets started, it will be much, much easier than she ever would have thought possible. The earth has been softened by weeks of unseasonably warm weather and the recent rains sweeping in mean the soil surrenders with ease as the spade cuts and carves. Yes, a certain degree of force and perseverance are needed to dig deep enough, to outwit the foxes and other scavengers, and she is breathless and sweating. But she is breathless and sweating anyway.

Her thoughts drift. Before she can stop herself, a mirthless bubble of mucus bursts, unbidden, from between her bitten and bleeding lips. The bubble is frothy, bloodsoaked. She swallows the bitter taste away and wipes blood, sweat and clay from her brow.

This is the easy part. She still hasn't looked, won't look. The body. It is terrible. Torn. She continues.

The first drops of rain hit the back of her neck as she grasps under the arms and drags the body to the edge. Within seconds she is drenched and shivering, with the cold, the rain, the exertion, the realization.

It doesn't take long. Not really. A momentary panic as she can't find the second shoe. Then she spies it, half-submerged, heel pointing upwards out of the clay like an exotic scarlet spur.

Eight
He can't put his finger on it. He just knows.

The door into the hall is closed. Apprehensive that he is trailing slush and mud across her immaculate oak floor, he grasps the handle. It gives crisply under minimal pressure and the beyond emerges. Sitting on the carpet in self-confident isolation, a suitcase adorned with stickers from around the world. Paris, Berlin, Antigua, New Zealand. Sophie's suitcase. He knows this because Annie has never left the country. Annie has a fear of flying so profound that she will never contemplate even the remote possibility. *Rather stick needles in my eyes* she has said to Roy on more than one occasion.

Despite a curiosity that surprises him, Roy cannot bring himself to go further, to cross the expanse of plush carpet. He clears his throat gruffly and calls Annie's name, this time louder, with growing assurance that it doesn't matter because she is not here.

Nine

It lies, crumpled. Face down. The body. This is how she thinks of it now. Not Sophie. Just 'body' as if it has nothing at all to do with her. Annie had intended to lie it flat at the bottom, arms folded across chest, a modicum of decorum, respect for the deceased. It was the very least she could do. But as she half leaned, half clambered into the grave, the walls began to crumble and collapse. She was forced to leave the body where it fell. Face down. Eating earth.

She pauses, waits for her breath to steady, the hammering in her chest to lessen. She kneels forward, brings the shoes together tenderly as if a sacred relic and places them on top of the inert bulk below. The soles make a small clacking sound which is instantaneously lost as the rain falls harder.

Ten

Roy has no right to be here. He knows the house is empty, that there is nothing to be gained, nothing to see. He returns to the back door and steps outside, closing the door behind him. No business here at all, regardless of a murmur or tickle or itch or … he doesn't know what. Best if he goes home. He can always pop along again tomorrow, weather permitting. Better still, phone Annie on her landline before setting off. Let her know he's intending to drop by if it suits her.

He pushes his gloves on and tramps towards the gate. The darkening sky is cloud-full. More snow, he thinks. Better get a move on. It is as he is about to turn the corner that he articulates his disquiet.

The spade.

Lying there. Not put away, not positioned where it belongs. Inside. With the rakes. Hoes. Edging iron. Forks. Trowels. Ranked in order of size, hanging on nails with military precision. Standing to attention.

Eleven

Hands blistering, raw, Annie knows she must get rid of her clothes, with their blood splashes and brain spatters. She pulls them away from her sodden flesh, throws them into the pit and heaps soil onto the mound with bare hands. The sky is black as pitch, rain is turning to hail and high in the sky fireworks dance and sing to welcome the new year. Hearing them she begins to cry.

Still the hail is driving, the sleet is sheeting down.

She finishes. Gasping, retching. She drags the spade over to the side of the shed where she leaves it, leaning, leering. She crawls her way back to where the body of her child lies entombed. She sits, cross-legged as if about to pray. A vile vigil.

She is naked. Shivering. Black dirt under nails. She closes her eyes. Realises. The buzzing. The buzzing has stopped. She howls.

At some point she sleeps.

It is the absence of sound that brings her back. The silence. That and the seeping chill through saturated skin. The first thing she sees as she opens her eyes is the swing hanging. Blood stars and snow mingle as they fall.

Twelve

He crosses to the shed. The snow has drifted and is above his knees, but the spade announces itself never-the-less. It is filthy. Mud, clay, leaves, grass, cling to every inch of red-rimmed, red-crusted steel.

This is not Annie. Annie would never leave a spade un-wiped, un-clean. Everything is cleaned. Everything is wiped. Put away respectfully in the proper place. Everything.

Roy looks out again over the darkening landscape. He has a matter of minutes before the sun drops below the hill, and visibility is lost. .He runs his gloved finger along the edge of the spade, transferring the red rimmed matter to his hand. He looks closer. At what he thinks it might be but cannot believe it is.

He sets off across the lawn towards Sophie's swing, the cruelly coiled chain, the deformed red seat, motionless as the lengthening shadows contrast with the last of the sun's rays.

Shine. Shadow.

Roy is a rational man. A thoughtful man. Considered and methodical. He feels ridiculous. For want of something to distract him he extends his hand and gently pushes the red seat back and forth. The snow slides off, hitting the ground with a crunch. He glances down. A few feet away he sees chicken bones sticking out of the snow. Brittle, blue chicken bones.

He frowns. Leans. Looks again. Crouches down and gently brushes away the soft snow from around Annie's frozen fingers.

Oh sweet Jesus, no. Not this. Not like this. He scrabbles and digs and claws and scrapes until her face, mouth, are clear of dirt and snow. Her eyes are closed, face white, skin translucent, lips blue. A little finger poised as if mocking.

Thirteen

It is nine days before the daughter is reported missing, the realisation that no-one has seen her since before the holiday. Nine days before they return, dig down, dig deeper and the earth reveals another secret among the bulbs that have taken root with fledgling shoots. A pair of red soled shoes with pointy stab heels, turning upwards to seek the light.

Author's note: My short story was developed in late 2018, a few months after joining the Manchester Irish Writers' group. One evening I anxiously submitted the first chapter to the group for critique. It is without doubt thanks to their positive, thoughtful and honest comments that I decided to persevere with the story. Until I met the group, I didn't really believe that I could write – that I had anything to say. Their support, encouragement, friendship and wealth of experience as individuals and as a group, has continued to inspire me.

PAT McALEESE

Pat joined the Manchester Irish Writers in 2017. Originally from Belfast, she came to Manchester in 1969 to take up a three-year teacher training course, at Sedgley Park College of Education, and has taught in Belfast, the Bahama Islands and locally in Manchester, in a long and varied teaching career. She feels that by joining the Manchester Irish Writers she learned from more experienced writers and benefitted from the positive and encouraging feedback on her own fledgling attempts; enough to give her the impetus and confidence to write a children's novel, *Cassie and the Howling Banshee*. She is also in the process of completing a second. Her story *Crossing Over in 1969* was shortlisted in the King Lear Prizes competition in the Real Story category. A mother to four grown up children and grandmother to seven grandchildren she now considers Manchester to be "home from home."

WALLS
Bare lies the waste of deserted houses,
A no man's land, where no man can live,
The barbed wire fence gets higher and higher,
A polarised community refuses to give,
And murals on the gable walls,
Show from the Shankill to the Falls.
A different story, a different creed,
Depicting struggles, or heroic deeds.
Within each side, the children play,
They go to school, they even pray
For peace and love and harmony,
And care towards God's family.

The foreign faces in the town,
Are welcomed in, they earn their pound,

Their children know no hatred there,
It's not their war and not their care.
They don't take sides or understand,
The nature of this complex land,
With green and gold or red and blue,
To them it's all afresh and new.
And things look pretty normal here,
The schools are nice, the people dear.

But scratch beneath the surface please,
These walls are high, this air so free,
Abounds with muted mistrust still,
Despite agreements, laws and bills,
And people here are slow to change,
They've seen too much, they keep their range
Of friendships down to what they know,
Don't roam too far or try to grow,
Just stay within these walls so high,
Afraid to live, afraid to die.

Author's note: Coming from Belfast and seeing the political situation deteriorate over the years, it was particularly sad on my frequent visits back home to see the barricades going up between the two communities, metaphorically speaking at first and then literally. Walls were built higher and higher between the Catholic and Protestant communities living in flashpoint areas. My poem describes both types of walls; one as a mindset and the other as a physical barrier.

CROSSING OVER IN 1969

The year 1969 was a momentous year for lots of reasons. To the rest of the world, it was the year when Neil Armstrong uttered those famous words which would be written into history books for generations to come.

"That's one small step for man. One giant leap for mankind."

Everyone was glued to their small black and white televisions, 650 million viewers the world over, and watched in awe, as these astronauts made their moon landing in the Apollo lunar module, and stepped out onto the pale, barren, rocky, silent and desolate landscape that no man had ever stepped on before.

But 1969 was also a momentous year for me on two different levels; not just about what was happening in our world or even our universe, but what was happening in *my* life, *my* city and *my* world. Was there a seismic shift in the atmosphere in 1969, when there were so many student demonstrations in Paris and in England for example? What was it about that year that stands out for me in so many ways and for so many reasons? Well, I was eighteen, I had just left school and was waiting for the results of my 'A' levels to decide in which direction my life would take me, and most of my friends who were all at that point in life, were doing exactly the same thing.

There had been unrest in Belfast and in Derry, as the civil rights movement got underway copied from their black counterparts in the United States, and singing "We Shall Overcome," they made their way in peaceful marches, through the Catholic towns of Coalisland, and the centre of Derry, just as they had on the streets of Alabama and Atlanta Georgia. The marchers in Northern Ireland also carried banners calling for "One Man, One Vote" but had been met with hostility and aggression by the police just as they had on the streets of Atlanta. Here too in Northern Ireland, peaceful protestors had been battened, water hosed, had rubber bullets fired at them, and were tear gassed. The subsequent rioting that had ensued, left whole areas battle scarred, with burnt out cars, broken glass and broken up pavements. On the British national news at six o clock, English journalists who were flying over to Northern Ireland in droves stood on the streets of Belfast and asked the question.

"Why is this happening?"

"What do they mean when they say one man one vote?"

Because until this moment in 1969, no-one in the rest of Britain let alone Europe, realised that what existed in England, Scotland and Wales did not exist in Northern Ireland; there was no real democracy. Boundaries were gerrymandered in order to achieve a Protestant unionist majority, even in areas like Derry which had a majority of Catholics living there. The population in Derry had little representation in Stormont, because as James Craig the first prime minister of Northern Ireland from 1943-63 had said quite proudly, "We have a Protestant government for a Protestant people" and thought that after fifty years of being in power that would remain the case forever. He also said that he wouldn't even employ a Catholic gardener to cut the grass around the Stormont building.

Against this backdrop of unrest and fear and rioting, something happened in 1969 that is forever etched in my memory. It was August, and a clear summer's evening when my friend Isobel and I decided to walk to visit our other friend Therese who lived less than a quarter of a mile away. I can well remember trying to break in some new black patent shoes, and moaning about a sore heel all the way there, and my poor long suffering friend having to put up with me. In the days before mobile phones, you were never quite sure if you caught someone in or not and as luck would have it (or not) Therese had gone for a driving lesson, but her father assured us that as she shouldn't be too long, we could come in and wait for her. We noticed his brand new, white saloon car parked outside and were envious that Therese an only child, whose mother had not long died before, would soon be driving it, when she passed her driving test. We chatted to her father, but after waiting an hour or so we thought that Therese had gone somewhere else after her lesson, and as it was now 10 o' clock and beginning to get dark, we decided to venture home and see Therese another time. We chatted idly as we strolled down the main road at our leisure and reached the crossroad on the way. We had just stepped across to the other side when some shots rang out and the bullets hit the wall to our left just above our heads. I remember seeing the bullet holes, and the realisation that we had just escaped being shot, and then I remembered running as fast as I could in a blur, completely forgetting that my new shoes were killing me, and seriously doubting that if Mary Peters the Olympian athlete, had tried to race me that evening, that I would have been beaten. Of course, thankfully, we reached home safe and sound, and with a stitch in my side I wondered for a split second if I was hit. I also wondered if we were the intended target, or if the gunman had a bad aim, but I guess we didn't hang around long enough to find out. Nevertheless, we were glad to be alive, as unfortunately ricochet bullets could also kill, as we heard daily on the news bulletins. I survived, and so did my brand new black patent shoes.

However, the next morning on the local news which everyone listened to almost as a necessity, we heard that the street we had just visited the night before had been burned to the ground. The whole street! As I said, we just left

Therese's house in Bombay Street, at about ten o' clock, but after midnight, just two hours later, gangs of Protestants led by the reserve police (better known as the B Specials) who lived among them in their community close by, in retaliation for the rioting that had been taking place against the police (a force mainly made up of loyalists and protestants), had decided to ethnic cleanse the areas which ran parallel to theirs. Those reserve police, who were meant to be the protectors of the whole community, held the residents back while their homes were burned to the ground. That brand new white car we had been admiring the night before, had been used unsuccessfully as a barricade to keep the marauders out. It was now a burnt-out shell like the rest we saw from time to time, before the bulldozers came in to clear them. We also heard on the news that the people who lived in Bombay Street, were left homeless, and had to go to a school hall, or a neighbour's for that night, and subsequent nights, until they could all be accommodated elsewhere. We were desperate to hear any news of Therese and her father, but heard nothing. We had no idea where she was. However, two days later Therese came to my house. It was a relief to see that she was alright, but unfortunately, the Therese I spoke to was a changed person.

She was so angry at the 'B' Specials, but she also desperately wanted me to go with her to help her to try to find something, anything, which she could salvage from her home. As we walked along the main Falls Road, the atmosphere was charged and electric with a feeling of gloom and darkness, pervading the very air we breathed. The smoke and smells hung on every cloud, the aftermath of the incidents of the previous nights. Even those police standing on each corner looked edgy and ill at ease. Therese had to be pulled away from verbally abusing them by me, but after what she had witnessed and experienced who could have blamed her?

When we got to her house, the sight which met me was something I shall never forget. I imagined, well I sort of pictured, a shell of a house and the remnants of a whole street still there. Instead, very low walls edged a sea of rubble which stretched all the way down the long road as far as the eye could see. It looked like the Luftwaffe had completely blitzed it from above and I was so stunned and shocked and completely immobile as I stared at this cataclysmic sight, while Therese, who had obviously seen all of this two nights before, and lived through it, stepped gingerly over the low wall of what had been her home, and bent down to begin lifting rubble, and turn bricks over, to find something, anything to remind her of her mother. I was in awe of her courage, but I was no use at all to her, as my eyes blurred with tears, but I bent down anyway and tried to search frantically too. Therese was more angry than I had ever seen her before, but stoic, and her determination was rewarded with a piece of a gold cross and chain that she recognised as her late mother's. She held onto it and looked up at the sky in gratitude.

So, as Neil Armstrong on July 20th in 1969, stepped onto a rocky, barren, cold landscape on a journey that the rest of mankind would never ever forget; by choice, Therese without choice; just a few weeks later, on 15th August 1969, stepped onto the barren, rocky, pale and cold space, which had encapsulated her every memory, her whole waking life in total, for the previous eighteen years. A small moment in time, but a momentous night which changed the lives of all of those friends and neighbours who lived there, fifty years ago, that none of *us* would ever, ever forget.

Author's note: I wrote this story in response to a themed writing exercise in 2019. This was deemed to be part of the Manchester Irish Centre's portfolio of events in order to celebrate St. Patrick's Day that year and was to be originally entitled Crossing Over. *However, because it coincided with the 50ᵗʰ anniversary of the tumultuous events which took place in Belfast in August 1969, I changed the title to* Crossing Over *in 1969, to remember my friend Therese RIP, and what she and her neighbours experienced that dreadful night in Belfast.*

WHAT'S IN A NAME?

My brother Dermot, eight years my senior, was an avid reader. So much so, that he could usually be seen hunched over the fire with his book in hand, oblivious to everything and everyone around him. Even at mealtimes, he could be seen eating and reading at the same time, as he turned over the pages of his book, until he was told off by my mother, and the book was put to one side. Once, when I was going to the library, he asked me to bring back a John Steinbeck book for him. I guess that the author's name was a little bit unusual for me (as a five- or six-year-old) to remember, so I decided to repeat the name "Steinbeck, Steinbeck," over and over again to myself, as I skipped gaily along down to the Central Library in Belfast, down Castle Street, across Millfield, down Upper Library Street, and round the corner to the library, which usually took fifteen to twenty minutes. In those days we were quite "free range" kids who did things by themselves and *for* themselves quite independently.

On the way, I always made an effort to stop and stare into the pet shop window in Montgomery Street. There, puppies vied with kittens for space, and tumbled around in full view

93

of the public, all for sale to *anyone*, so the footpath outside was usually crowded with children all *oohing* and *aahing*. But everyone's favourite act was that of the monkeys, who never failed to entertain the public with their antics. So unfortunately, by the time I reached the library and found my own books, which were usually fairy tales by Andrew Lang, the name Steinbeck had completely left my head. As I approached the librarian at the counter, I heard myself asking, "Have you any books written by Einstein?" completely oblivious to the look of complete shock my words received.

The librarian was a very large middle-aged lady with round glasses perched on the end of her nose. "Einstein?" she repeated incredulously as she looked around to the other librarians behind her to catch their attention. They turned from what they were doing, amused and surprised in equal measure.

Then the very large imposing lady at the front of the desk, leaned over and in hushed tones asked, "Who?" and followed by a long pause, she repeated, *"Who, might I ask, wants a book written by Einstein?"*

"Oh," I shrugged quite nonchalantly, "Why, my big brother, Dermot of course." I answered as if she should know this, and that he read scientific books every day, and that I was well used to bringing them home.

"Well!" she breathed out quite quickly, but she recovered herself sufficiently, to make her way round to the other side of the counter towards me.

"Now, which one my dear?" she spoke quite reverently to me, as though I had suddenly grown in stature, which I'd never noticed before in all my previous visits. "The theory of relativity?" she queried.

Not really having a clue as to what she was referring to, and having absolutely no inkling of what this great scientist had achieved or what his theories were, I decided to play it safe. I nodded as if I knew all about this famous man, as I looked up at this large foreboding, but now suddenly congenial lady. She took my hand, and I found myself being led down the non-fiction aisles. Now these were an unknown entity to me, as I always gravitated towards the children's section, and headed straight for Andrew Lang's multi coloured fairy stories. I had worked my way practically across the whole shelf, the Blue Fairy Book, the Yellow, the Green and so on, therefore the adult non-fiction area was a completely unknown territory to me. She pointed to huge tomes and volumes still asking me questions, but of course this was no help to me at all. I settled for one of Einstein's books that she recommended, not really caring or understanding its significance, and quickly exited the building as fast as my little legs could carry me, still receiving admiring glances from the librarians as I did so.

Back home Dermot laughed out loud with his head thrown back as he often did, clearly very amused by the whole episode, but he did read through the book and then asked. "Where did you hear the name Einstein?"

Author's note: Looking back, I must have looked like a child prodigy or a relation of one anyway to the librarians and years later, when I read the book Matilda *to my class, it never failed to make me smile, and remind me of my very undeserved Matilda moment.*

AN EXTRACT FROM *CASSIE AND THE HOWLING BANSHEE*

One still night, a few weeks later, when the sky was so clear and black it throbbed with stars and the waxing moon shone silver over the treetops, Cassie heard a strange cry again. At first, she thought it was a fox trying to get into the hen house, but usually when that happened the hens would let out wild screeches and the rooster would crow loud and clear as a warning. There were no sounds coming from the hen house, and the crying, almost wailing sounds seemed to grow closer and closer and louder and louder till Cassie sprang out of bed to peer through the window. There, sitting on the low wall that separated the garden from the vegetable patch, sat a little old lady combing her thin white hair over her shoulder as she stared up at the house. Cassie sucked in her breath as the shock registered in the pit of her stomach.

"A banshee?" she questioned herself. "No, no, we don't want you back here again." She rushed downstairs as quickly and as quietly as she could, wondering why no-one else seemed to hear the strange wailing and crying. She unlocked the back door as her heart raced in her chest and her hands shook with fear. She stepped out just as the banshee rose into the air, and as she did so, her hair spread all around her head like a green fan, and her skin which was pale and translucent pulsated and changed colours as she continued to wail. First her face glowed a pale blue, and then a bright red, before it changed back again to a sickly green. Cassie stood transfixed, mesmerised and frozen to the spot, gradually becoming aware that she was witnessing a phenomenon and a legend so real and alive, that she felt she could almost touch it with an outstretched hand.

Author's note: Set in the Mourne mountains (my favourite place in the whole wide world), in the early part of the twentieth century, Cassie and the Howling Banshee *encompasses the folklore I grew up with, and describes the quest the hero has to undergo to help her mother get the medical help she needed. I originally wrote this story for my English grandkids to familiarise them with their Irish heritage and I included some of their names in the story; for example, Tara, Emmet and Theodora, and various other relative's names like Alanna, Brigid, Gerard and Eileen in order to engage them. I then decided to self-publish the book on* Amazon, *found the experience very enjoyable, and started writing a sequel,* Cassie and the Pesky Pooka Fairies, *which I'm in the process of completing. The kids have been very positive in their response – so far!*

MARY McGONAGLE

Mary comes from Malin in Co Donegal. She writes under her maiden name of Mary McGonagle. She joined the Manchester Irish Writers' group when she retired from teaching. She had dabbled a bit in writing, but needed some feedback, so was delighted when she found the group. Once she joined, she found them very welcoming and encouraging. Their feedback was very useful too.

A few years ago Mary returned to Donegal and continued her writing, but continued her contact with the group. She feels very grateful for the support of the Manchester Irish Writers, where her writing journey began.

FUTTING TURF

Last night I dreamt I was futting turf,
A dream so vivid, a memory real.
School holiday in the moss.
Bending over, picking up.
Four together, standing straight.
Rough and dry,
Stinging hands.
Sun burns, no cream.
Midges biting, turf mould
Blinding eyes.
'Good drying weather,'
Someone says
Secretly I hope for rain
And going home.
'You cannot leave
'Till work is done.'
Later, running home,

Through coarse heather,
Legs scorched,
Face black, eyes blind,
Waking up relieved.
Memory washes over me.
Reminding me that it was
Only a bad dream.

Author's note: This poem is self-explanatory. It was inspired by memories of my school holidays spent on the moss. Futting turf was a hateful job, the poem emphasises the relief I found when I realised I was only dreaming.

MY HOME PLACE

Holiday time comes around again
Plans are made, flights are booked
People go away to exotic places
Where the sun shines every day
I feel a little envious and wish that
I was going somewhere exciting too.

Instead, I am stuck at here at home
I feel restless and decide to wander outside.
It's beginning to grow dark now,
As I look around me I think of those places
Where my friends were enjoying right now.

I stand there in the silence of the evening
The light is beginning to fade now and
The sky is developing a pinkish hue
A crescent moon adds magic to the scene.
The hawthorn tree nearby wafts its scent.

As I stand here wrapped in its perfume

A tranquil peace begins to drop and I'm
suddenly.
Awake to the beauty of this my place.
I have no regrets of having to stay here -
In my home place.

Author's note: This poem was inspired by the beauty surrounding me. I am lucky enough to live in a very scenic part of Donegal. One evening as I was looking out of my window and longing for foreign climes it just occurred to me how amazing my own home was.

DONEGAL TO MANCHESTER

In the year of sixty-four
With great excitement and furore
I packed my bag and took it all
Far away from Donegal
Off to Manchester I did go
To find a job and make some dough
But at night I could not sleep,
Even when I counted sheep
The hustle bustle of the night
Cars and buses, city lights,
Kept me awake till dawn of day
I thought of home and making hay
Queues of people all around ,
Wait for buses city-bound
Rushing here rushing there
Not a minute could they spare.
Going about their daily labour,
No time to talk to any neighbour
Here was me a country girl
With my mind all in a whirl

Thoughts of home and open doors
Where people stop and chat for hours
But very soon I did adapt
I had to change the way I spoke
From saying aye, and noh, and very apt
I learned the tae was called the tea
Something was small instead of wee
I brushed the floor and not the flure
And shut the door and not the dure
I never stopped to have a chat,
For people had no time for that

Now when I go home again
People say it's very plain
The way I speak is not the same
Now when I'm here I ask for tea,
Then back home it is to tae.

Author's note: This poem arose from reminiscing about when I first left Donegal to go to Manchester and culture shock that ensued, particularly relating to the linguistic differences!

KEVIN McMAHON

Kevin joined the group in 1998, having won the New Writing Award at Listowel Writers' Week. Professional commitments took him away between 2003 and 2013, when he rejoined, shortly before our 20th anniversary. While he has since been shortlisted for the Fish Short Memoir Prize and the Short Story Award, most of Kevin's recent writing has been for the stage. A short verse-drama developed as part of the group's Somme Centenary event was a finalist in the Kenneth Branagh International Drama Writing Award. Now developed to full-length, the play – *The Claykickers' Chorus* – was due to run for a month in London, when covid closed the theatres in 2020. A new production of the piece – and a UK tour – is planned, by the production company who purchased the rights, Wild Thyme Productions.

Kevin also wrote a musical – *Punchy* – in collaboration with musician Jack Terroni, which ran for four weeks in The Courtyard Theatre, Hoxton, in 2021. Other plays have been staged in Liverpool, Salford and Birmingham, as well as performances at the Oldham Coliseum and Wolverhampton's Arena Theatre.

SONGS HE LEFT UNSUNG (MONOLOGUE)

> "And here where that sweet poet sleeps
> I hear the songs he left unsung."
> *At a Poet's Grave* by Francis Ledwidge (1887-1917)

[A recording of John McCormack singing When You and I Were Young *plays as the scene opens. Maggie enters. She is a pale woman possibly thirty years old but looking ten*

102

years older. She holds a framed photograph of two men, at which she frequently looks, occasionally addressing the image of her husband. The song fades.]

My Jackie had the voice of an angel. God I wish you could have heard him! He'd close his eyes, and God you'd think it was the voice of Count John McCormack his self. "When you and I were young" – that was his special one for me. His Maggie. He'd sing it to me softly at night and I tell you I'd go weak when I heard him! We dreamed of growing old together – like in the song. Together in our new country – "our new *free* Ireland" he said it would be.

That was his other favourite one – everyone used be asking him to sing it – "A Nation Once Again". He'd stand there, and his arms doing all the actions. When it said "boyhood's fire burned in my blood" wasn't his fist clenched over his heart. Then he'd pull his two hands apart to show "fetters rent in twain". He loved that song.

I swear, I never heard a better singer.

He was a real patriot. Much good it did him. He worshipped Mister Redmond - took it *all* in. About Home Rule being promised as soon as the war was done, I mean. And *Monsignor* Morrissey giving out from the pulpit about "poor little *Catholic* Belgium", and the Germans cutting the hands off the little childer and violating nuns and all. It'd bring tears to a glass eye.

"Maggie," says he, "I'm going to enlist. It's me duty," he says. And I was sad, but I was *so* proud of him. His brother went along with him to sign up in the Fusiliers. Brendan. He was only nineteen, but he doted on Jackie, and Jackie was like a father and a brother to him, since their own father died.

That's the two of them there.

It'd melt the heart of you to see them in their uniform.

The day they left Dublin – God you should have seen it! They was on the way to Westland Row to go on training in Cork. The roads was lined with people cheering them on, even though the rain was hopping off the streets. Our brave lads off to do their duty.

We was just a year married that day. I saw him as he passed, and weren't they singing it as he went by – "A Nation Once Again" – wasn't it the Dubs' regimental song. And the smile on him! You could hear his voice above the whole lot of them.

It was the last time I ever heard him sing.

It was the last time I saw him smile.

Well no sooner were the decent men gone, when those *gurriers* came out of the woodwork. Them and their German guns. The Volunteers.

Hardly no one supported them, you know, with their so-called Rising. No one could believe that after so long playing at soldiers, drillin' with their hurleys and brush handles, they'd *actually* start firing on their own. D'you know there were Dublin Fusiliers defending the city that week – lads like my Jackie. Not that that lot cared who was in the way when they loosed off their guns.

When they was beaten, they was marched through the streets, and the women lined up and pelted them with stones and rotted fruit. I did meself. Carrying on like that while our men was fighting and dying in the trenches.

I didn't know that day how close to the truth that was.

It was that same week. Jackie was in a place called Loos. In France. They was in the trenches and saw this cloud spreading towards them, he said. They thought it was gas, so they all put on their masks, and waited. They was sure the Germans would attack.

Well nothing happened. One of the men says that it's just smoke. That's all it was as well, so off come the masks. Then a couple of hours later, doesn't the same thing happen. They don't bother with the masks this time.

But this time it's gas. Chlorine.

It killed Brendan. Jackie got his mask on, but not before a bit of the gas had got to his lungs. Then he found Brendan – further up the trench.

He never told me anything else about it. God love him, he wanted to save me that. But I knew.

I knew how horribly poor Brendan suffered before he drowned in the foam from his lungs. I knew ... I knew what *haunted* him. I heard him yelling in the night, you see. Whenever he *managed* to get some sleep, he was trying to save his little brother, screaming as he watched him choke. Again and again. Night after night. Can you *imagine* what....? Watching him tortured every time he ....? Once I

105

tried to speak to him, but the *look*...! I never tried again – but I knew.

So the same week those *patriotic* Irishmen were firing their German guns on honest Dubliners, their German friends were tricking our husbands, our sons, to choke them.

Well Jackie spent nearly a month in a field hospital while he got better from the gas he'd taken in. But he never recovered. Oh, he was up and walking, and went back to the Front, but *inside* he was killed with Brendan. He never forgave himself for not dying right there beside him in the trench, Brendan signing up as he did because of him.

It was like two ghosts came home to me.

He was at Passchendaele later. 1917 it'd be. He got wounded again there – some shrapnel in his leg. He was sent home then. The Spring of 1918.

When the ship came into North Wall, there was hundreds of people there, mainly women. All these men were being helped off the ship – blind, some of them, some without legs. And do you know what they did? They threw stones at them! Stones and insults! They yelled names at them – "Cowards. Traitors." Could you believe that? And some of them the very same ones who'd stood with me and yelled when the Volunteers was pelted.

The *bitches*! The bloody *hypocrites!* My Jackie was as strong a patriot as any one of them gobshites!

Well it took him a long while to be fit to look for work. Nothing like the labouring he'd done before, you know. He wasn't strong enough for that. And it wouldn't have

106

mattered if he was. There was no work for someone who'd served in the British Army. Either the bosses was republicans and wouldn't have him in, or they was too scared of the republicans. Scared of their buildings being burned. Or worse.

And the priests? They did nothing to help! They soon forgot all the things they'd said to make fellas like Jackie sign up.

"God'll reward him Maggie," says Monsignor Morrissey... Some reward!

It was me sister asked would we come over here and join her. She'd been in Ancoats since before the war. There was work in the cotton mills that time. We had the bit of money the British gave Jackie – to stop him joining the rebels. So we could meet the fare, and we came late in 1919.

He was as good as run out of the country he loved!

Well I got work but he never did. His chest was weak from the gas, you see. He *hated* to see that! Thought he'd failed me – no matter what I said. "Get yourself strong," I'd tell him, "and you'll soon be working." But I think we both knew .... He was too weak. And he was exhausted - he never slept more than an hour at a time before the terrors woke him. So when the flu came he couldn't fight it.

At least he *didn't* fight it. And try as I might, I couldn't make him. He got sick one day, and two days later he was gone.

God knows what he'd think of what's going on over there now! They have their so-called Treaty and their *"Free State"*, and they've turned on each other. Again! Well they're welcome to it, bad cess to the lot of them!

Ah, Jackie love, a Nation once again. Not what we dreamed of is it?

[She continues to look at the picture, and quietly, haltingly at first, starts to sing in a cracked voice no longer used to song]

'I wandered today to the hill…. Maggie
To watch the scene below
The creek and the creaking old mill Maggie
As we used to long long ago…'

[The singing tails off]

I *wish* you could have heard him sing!

[The recording of John McCormack's version fades up, at the last verse:

'And now we are aged and grey, Maggie
And the trials of life nearly done
Let us sing of the days that are gone Maggie
When you and I were young.'

FADE]

Author's note: The group received funding to celebrate our 20th anniversary and decided to stage a series of monologues marking 200 years of Irish immigration to Manchester. A seminar in monologue-writing kick-started

the project, and changed my writing journey forever. Songs
He Left Unsung *was the first script I had ever written. Since
the* Changing Skies *production, the monologue has been
staged in Salford, Liverpool and Wolverhampton.*

AFTERMATH

Manchester 23.5.2017

In the green glow of Whitworth Park
students bristle with mid-exam frenzy
of relaxation and feigned normality.
A yellow frisbee scutters between trees
then trundles to where a woman sits
on tartan square in leaf-shade.
Her child crawls across the rug,
recoils at each edge when he feels
the cool prick of grass.
The mother smiles but cannot
quell the gall of dread,
One day, this child will feel his way
beyond these narrow boundaries;
will want to join his friends
in happy concert crowds,
with appeasing - meaningless -
promises of care; will step
beyond the limits of her care.

*Author's note: This was an immediate response to the awful
events on 22 May 2017, when a suicide bomber killed
concert-goers in the MEN Arena. Writing can be an attempt
to create sense out of the senseless, and at our next meeting
we found that several of the Writers had independently been
moved to create something. A collection of the poems
produced by the group was added to the impromptu*

memorial in St Ann's Square, honouring those murdered that dreadful night.

THE SET

Hilversum. That was where I would settle. Its very name sang of possibilities and enchantment, a landscape of dramatic, sun-flecked heights, I was sure; of silver lakes, steeped in adventure, but with the solidity and security of lush, green lowlands reflected in that final syllable. That was the place for me. It was no rushed or impulsive decision: I had a brief dalliance with Droitwich before deciding it was probably too inhospitable a desert for my long-term composure. And Daventry too, but I dismissed that as Father Quigley-on-the-Missions had died with something that sounded alarmingly similar. No, it was Hilversum for me.

My atlas was the dial of the Bush radio – "The Set" as it was known in our house. It perched, like an all-knowing owl, on a solid, purpose-built shelf beneath the Sacred Heart picture that leaned out from our kitchen wall. The position of the shelf was dictated by two considerations: firstly, it had to be high enough to allow us to sit on the bench below at the back of the kitchen table, without our heads being injured, or, I suspect more importantly, disrupting the tuning. The second reason was to allow The Set to share the same single plug socket with the Sacred Heart lamp, via a distinctly unsafe-looking adapter cube.

The proximity of The Set to the picture meant that only a short leap of imagination was required to fancy that the image actually intoned the words of the RTE weather forecast each evening. In fact, that is not so far-fetched, as the Sacred Heart himself was perhaps the only figure imbued with authority equal to the RTE weather forecaster. The shelf had been erected in advance, and we children had speculated wildly about its purpose. I had my heart set on a parrot's cage, but my sister, Bernadette, a gentle reverent soul, had decided, entirely without imagination or adventure in my opinion, that it would be for flowers to be placed before the Sacred Heart. I devoutly prayed that she was wrong.

When the day came, my father processed into the house with the wireless set, and we were speechless with excitement and anticipation. The latter was quickly diluted when we were told, in no uncertain terms, that touching it would be regarded as an act of treachery! My father plugged it in and turned the switch. We listened. Nothing. A surge of disappointment washed over us, until slowly a hiss filled the room. A faint yellow glow illuminated the dial, and from the dark sheen of the central panel appeared a dimly-lit litany of locations, a world of opportunity. My father flexed his fingers, like a surgeon, and placed forefinger and thumb on either side of the brown, Bakelite knob. He slowly turned it, and crystallising from the hiss came a squabble of alien voices, each rising then fading like a figure shouting on a moving carousel, to be replaced by a different, equally alien voice. Some female, but mostly male. All apparently solemn. A whine. Another hiss. He flexed his fingers again. Another turn, and suddenly words we recognised – the accent Irish, but not like our own; more like Bishop D'Arcy when he came to do the Confirmation, or the Dublin Redemptorists who did the Mission. The voices started to crackle, and fade, and my father quickly reversed the action until the declamatory tones were once again secured.

111

"Athlone!" my father announced. "The very man!"

Over the next few days, a number of our neighbours came in to see The Set. Appropriately admiring tones and nods of approval followed, apart from when P.J. stepped in.

"Oh," he said, squinting up at The Set. "'Tis only a Bush. Sure I have a Roberts, and it's grand!"

My mother made assuaging noises but I could tell my father was incensed. As P.J. left we were ushered out to play under the Big Tree, but we could hear the raised voice of my father, even as P.J. walked down the path to the road.

"What's a *'gobshite'* Bernadette?" I asked.

There followed a minor duel between the two men, to the frustration of my gentle-hearted mother, who always described P.J. as "a bit of a *stualán*, the poor lad". P.J., it transpired, genuinely believed, for two reasons, that he received the news headlines on the Roberts before we would get them on The Set: firstly, he believed, his equipment was superior; secondly, he lived geographically closer to Athlone than we did. The latter fact was undoubtedly true, as he lived on the road east past Pullamarla, but only a matter of a half-mile from us.

While not a daily occurrence, it was common to hear his voice shortly after the midday news and Angelus, breathlessly calling, "What do ye think of ....?" and expecting my father to be still blithely ignorant on the topic. My father on the other hand, took to rushing to the gateposts after the bulletin, waiting for any opportunity to shout to the approaching, sweating figure, "Isn't it a bad situation in Cuba?" – or whatever particular crisis he had absorbed. P.J.

never accepted defeat, putting his failure to prove his theory down solely to the inefficiencies of the brown jennet pulling the cart he drove, and later to the Raleigh bike, bought, my father insisted, specifically for the purpose of "bringing the old news"!

Apart from the news and weather bulletins, and the accompanying Angelus, The Set stood frustratingly mute, my father dismissing the daily offerings as "nothing else of the good". However, each Saturday, when he had gone off to Lahardane with Emmet and Billy the Line, my mother would fill the kitchen with music from "Ceili House". The driving strains of the Kilfenora, Tulla or Gallowglass Bands set feet tapping, and the gentle Galway accent of Seán Ó Murchú vied with a babble of voices from other nearby wavelengths, interrupting like incoherent drunks at the bar of Glennon's.

I would wait for the house to be empty, so that I could climb up onto the swaying bench, risking the reproachful glower of the Sacred Heart, and see more closely the possibilities beyond Athlone. The litany of exotic names thrilled me: Hamburg, Tallinn, Frankfurt AFN, Helsinki, Luxembourg, and there, Hilversum of my dreams. Occasionally, if I knew my parents would be gone some while, at a funeral perhaps, or bringing the cattle back from Cawley's Bog, I would turn the knob until it clicked and kindled the yellow glow. I would ease the tuning knob away from its habitual location braving the hiss and chatter of disapproval, as other voices emerged from the fog, interspersed occasionally with alien music. Carefully I inched the dial back to its resting place, though my father would invariably be able to tell that it had been interfered with.

"Someone," he would mutter darkly, "has been fiddling with The Set. I can hardly hear a word of the weather!" He then commenced his surgeon's adjustments to recapture the exact desired tuning.

My desire, however, was already stoked. That dial had cast a feeble yellow glimmer on a world of enticing places, beyond the townland; where life did not need to be anchored to Athlone; where, somewhere beyond our shores, lay Hilversum.

Author's note: One of the group's performances during the Irish Festival focused on the archive of artefacts held by the Irish World Heritage Centre in Manchester. My attention was captured by the large wireless set, so like one that dominated my upbringing! The piece was published in the Mining Memories *page of the* writing.ie *website and is stored in the Irish National Archive.*

OTTER BOARD

Bleached boots darkening
at each steady step
along the weed-pricked margins.
Left hand a blur,
flicking the crude frame to release
coils of hemp rope,
fed through coarse, white knuckle-crook
to take the taut line's strain.

That pike – they say –
was hung from the handlebars;
a hay-rope threaded though its gills,
savage mouth gaping.
Its tail swept the gravel

114

as the bike ticked back
along the sandroad, braced
against its dead weight.

Kiting out into the lough,
chisel-edged, poised
on its blade of lead,
the board draws out
its shoal of lures,
trailing their barbed irons
beyond the bank of reeds
in Ruane's Bay.

That mark etched on the table
shows where its snout had reached –
its ragged tail laid flush against the edge –
still visible in the barn's gloom,
if years' grime is smeared away.
The blackened, cobwebbed board
lies on it, wrapped around
with rotted hemp, and rust.

Author's note: Like The Set, *this was inspired by our reflections on traditional, and long-abandoned artefacts. My uncle in County Mayo made and used an otter board to fish local lakes for pike, and his skill in doing so was the stuff of local legend. This poem was written as a tribute to him, and a lament for rural crafts that have largely been consigned to history. As so often, its first airing was being shared with my fellow Manchester Irish Writers.*

LIMBO

The day Elvis died
I was home on holidays.

115

We scrambled over the bridge
To pick our way along the river
Until we got there.
A boundary-land, where parishes met
To shrug off their responsibilities.
Bee-laden air shrouded ground
Where unbaptised lay
Unforgettably ignored.
I asked her the name of this place:
"Srath na Leanbh" – The Child Field.
I tested those syllables,
My mouth sullenly awkward
She laughed at me.

She tested my old slender consonants
With the names of townlands:
"Aughalánsín," "Carrascehín,"
But each betrayed my flat
And faithless tongue;
Coarsened by Manchester streets,
Blunted by fear and fist.
I knew that moment
That I was in a boundary-land
Caught between tones
Of desire and necessity
And lost to both my worlds.

Author's note: Limbo *featured in Dr Liam Harte's 2017 publication,* Something About Home: New Writing on Migration and Belonging, *and arose from a series of workshops undertaken by Professor John McAuliffe with the group. The project combined work with writers' groups in Manchester, Castlebar and Belfast.*

ROSE MORRIS

Rose was born in Dungannon, Co. Tyrone, emigrated in 1970 to Manchester, where she settled, married and has two sons. After graduating from Belfast College of Art and Design she secured a Diploma in Art Education at the University of Birmingham and embarked on a career in Art and Design Education in Greater Manchester schools.

She is also a qualified Interior Designer and holds a Catholic Teacher's Certificate. She carried out Pastoral Care duties and Religious Instruction within Manchester schools.

She took early retirement in 1997 to pursue her own creative interests in painting, writing, photography, Irish cultural and caring projects both in Manchester and Ireland.

An active volunteer with Irish Community Care since it was founded in 1987, she served as a Trustee since 1992, holding various official roles on the Management Committee during that time, being Secretary from 1993 - 1996, Chair from 1996 - 2002 and again from 2015 - 2019 and was temporary Manager of Irish Community Care from April 2002 until February 2004,

Presently a Trustee of the Irish Diaspora Foundation and member of the Management Committee of the Irish World Heritage Centre. In her determination to promote Irish heritage, arts and culture she has initiated and coordinated many cultural and cross community events, international festivals and educational exchange programmes which included the EU Celtic Peoples Project and the East West educational initiative of the Good Friday Agreement.

She co-founded the Manchester Irish Writers in 1994 with Alrene Hughes and is Chair of the Management Committee but participates fully in workshops, popular events and promotions to ensure its successful continuance.

Her short stories, monologues and poetry have been included in the Manchester Irish Writers' publications; *The End of the Rodden, The Retting Dam, Stone of the Heart, Drawing Breath* and *Changing Skies* and in *Something about Home* by Liam Harte (2017).

THE FLAIL

My father threshed corn on winner nights
in the barn by the light of a hurricane lamp.
With his two branched flail rotating and landing
he flung onto sheaves the troubles of a long day.

Oat seeds rose and fell in a chasm golden,
and lashed the floor like rebounding hail.
Stalks softly crackled with each blow
to build a circular pile of chaffy grain.
A frightened cat darted back and forth
 keeping her distance from danger
but seeking still each escaping mouse.

A simple tool from ancient times
used to separate seeds from stalks,
Two slender branches from the elder,
held together with a thong of leather,
one the hand staff, one the swipple,
slung in circles to slash and scatter,
like Kubla Khan's fountain water.

DAILY BREAD

Soda bread, for her life itself
the first task of the day,
twice if there were visitors.
The windowed warmth
of the morning sun
and the heat from the fire
instilled a calming comfort
with a smell you could eat.

The first one cooling,
burnt deposits around the plate,
flour on her apron, jug,
churn and door knob.
Her marks unmistakable.
With a dusty turkey wing,
relic of a Christmas meal,
she brushed burnt flour
onto rising flames,
to send a shower of sparks
upward in the draught.

The soft dough knuckle flattened
into a hot oven, a knife pulled
over it in a cross of blessing.
A lid of glowing coals
lowered by tongs
with balanced hands,
and hung on the crook

I nestled in her lap
to watch and wait,
absorbing the grainy smell

the searing heat drew out
from the rising shape,
and the flour she has wiped
upon her apron.

TWISTING ROPES

Blistered hands
Soothed with spittle
to hold a grip
on glossy handles,
hollow branches of aa boor tree,
hooked bull wire,
piercing scented hay.

My father sat upon a straw bundle,
feeding hay into a spiralling centre.
My right hand circling
My left one held steady.
A step backwards
With each turn,
Holding taut the rope
Until I reached the garden wall.

CONTEMPLATIVE CONTENTMENT

(In memory of Sr. Nuala O'Connor. GS)

A fleeting visit to a contemplative sanctuary
Wiped away so much of a day gone wrong.
Composed in mind I took away a peace
Imparted through age and innocence,
Redress to the burdensome thoughts

Carried in from a material world.

From lives lived in love and prayer
A light into dark shadows of uncertainty.
A selfish corner of a hardened heart
Can but melt and soften in the calmness,
Relieving a spirit, battered and raw,
To go away revived and renewed.

There came with age an uncanny wisdom.
The struggle and search not in vain
Even when God's plan has blocked the way.
Those closest to that silence can only gain
From the strengths of those who stay behind,
Those who wait, those who contemplate.

THE RETTING DAM

In the upper field
a pond where duck
and downy feathers float.
Our icy slide in winter frost,
in summer our playground.
A dry webbed bed
we dug deep,
unearthed flax seed.
Relics of the linen trade.

Astride the brae ditch,
men sat, pipe smoke
adrift in a blue haze,
mingled memories.
The seed fiddle,
pulling boons.
retting smells,

drying spread,
lint and linseed,
scutching
and shouse.

SPARE THE ROD

The scythe sliced through the stalks of corn
laying low a swathe in a language of its own.
My father's boots left two grass trodden tracks
as they stepped along the sward.

I moved too, rod in hand,
to hold the heads aloft.
I kept apart from each long sweep
and held a distant reach.
Many thoughts went through my head
as the rasping cut spoke to me
with sounds and words attuned,
and I danced a step ahead of him
till we carried the 'Cailleach' home.

THE DOCTOR CALLS

The Littmann stethoscope,
his mark unmistakable
hangs around his neck.
Gladstone bag in hand
he climbs the stairs
to treat my father.
Bedridden with Farmer's Lung.
A lifetime of hay dust
now ingrained.
Fights for breath.

Inhaler hand rises and falls.

'Right John. how are you?
Let's have a look.
Take a deep breath.
And another one.
And another one.'
'There's a hundred and one remedies,
but no cure.'
A scribbled prescription,
only a Pharmacist could read,
torn noisily from a pad
and he is quickly gone.

*Author's note: A poem written at a workshop conducted
by John McAuliffe using found objects as a prompt. The
object given to me was a stethoscope.*

A SITTING EYE

I never saw her walk.
Just a one footed stride
Two crutches under her oxters.
Mouse grey hair held with a net.
I hold every line and smile on her face.
Anchor of my childhood
around which I toddled.
The only person who had time,
Listened,
told stories,
gave generously.
A figure I black
Absorbing the flames,
the gossip,
the noises of the house.

A battering crutch
signalled me to her side
to retrieve a lost hairpin,
a dropped spoon
or sort out her possessions
resting beside her on the hob.
Failing eyesight brought jewels in the sun
and monsters in the dark shadows.

In our boisterous play we stopped short
as she protected a bandaged leg
held outward on a low stool.
She liked *Bertie* to lick the wound.
"Healing in a dog's tongue", she said.

How had it happened?

After her death I learned.
It was the heel of my shoe.
My kicking foot as she nursed me.
While she lived I never knew.
She never let me.

BLASKET SOUND

I walk in early morning.
Climb breathless on a headland slope
Gulp blasts of sea brine and sandy dust
Carried on the mountain air.
Warmth of sunshine on my back,
orange to yellow as it rises higher.

Dew drenched grass parted with each step.
Reed hidden water gushing in ravines.

Froth from last night's rain on its back,
spreading slowly on a shining beach,
merging with waves from the incoming tide,
to swirl and twist in a sandy battle,
to die in a golden pebble bed.

Here as day dawns,
mountain, sea and man
meet in sun glazed mists,
Sheep and cows look on.
Birds swoop and dive.
The earth swept by sea air
and I am one with this.

A WIDOW WAITS

The balcony clad rooftops of Nantucket
pointed out by my son, 'Widow's Walks', he
said.
Boards that anxious wives of whaler's tread,
walked and watched, widows in waiting

.
My empathy leads me to walk in their shoes
as they continue to watch after no return.
Still gazing across the sea, all hope gone
but joined to a part of them buried in the
waves.

I think of widows I have known with wonder.
My pregnant grandmother widowed by the
Spanish Flu,
my niece widowed after a three-month
marriage
by a drunken driver on a Cavan Road.

I think of Synge's Widow Quin and her
playboy,
of the Windsor Widow's life of self-inflicted
mourning
and of my aunt Mary's widowhood predicted
at her wedding
from the rapid and separated rise from the altar
rails.

THAT TIME

I never spoke to my father on the telephone.
Never wrote him a letter-
The height of foolishness-
New-fangled things.
Never welcome in our house.
Few exchanges,
Rationed speeches,
Directives,
Requests,
Shared poetry,
Childhood memories.
History,
Euclid,
Latin responses.
Left school at eleven and took the spade.
But he had caught in a single room
All the knowledge imparted

To a schoolful of pupils
By a fearful man.

How do you till the land or harness a horse?
Learned that from Frank o' the burn.
Paddy McGuiness timed his watch

Using Old Moore's Almanac and the setting
sun.
Mark Patterson's cow calved.
It had two heads.
That was *before something* they said.
Uncle Edward had his house burned down.
He moved in after and evection.
There was a priest in every house that time.
They were taught Latin by a man beyond
Pomeroy.
Travelled there once a week on a bicycle.

Should have gone to America-
Kathleen, Maggie, Bridget and Charlie went-
Got as far as Cork, came back.

LANDING IN MANCHESTER

Birch Lane bedsit.
Wallpaper peeling,
from sloping ceilings
of an attic room.
A gurgling reaction
in the header tank
from a downstairs flush,
brings battering pipes,
and fading trickle.

A single light bulb
hangs on a dusty wire.
Bakelite switch dangles
above the bed.
A rusty gas ring coils
on a corner table.
Cooking odours lingering

in curtains and blankets.

First summer in a city,
in the heat of July.
A green grime clad
skylight window
filters a ray of sunlight
to a threadbare carpet,
rippled by floor boards,
worn away by the feet
of my predecessors … fellow emigrants.

Background music
from a portable radio
permanently tuned
to Radio Éireann.
Saturday's sponsors;
'Cakes by Gateau'
'The Kennedy's of Castleross'
Walton's record shop;
"If you feel like singing ….."

I dwell on recent news
of the first moon landing.
Broken on piped radio,
in the heat and fumes
of welded raincoats,
in a Cheetham factory.
"One small step... One giant leap"
My new space, a first step,
on my Manchester moon.

Author's note: Landing in Manchester *featured in Dr Liam Harte's 2017 publication,* Something About Home: New Writing on Migration and Belonging, *and arose from a series of workshops undertaken by Professor John McAuliffe with the group. The project combined work with writers' groups in Manchester, Castlebar and Belfast.*

PROCLAIM THE DREAM

Whether the dream was born in a herdsman's
shed
Or died in a stonebreaker's yard it still lives on
Through rhyme and reason in many a heart
A contested legacy or a revised history.

Some will look back and call it sublime
Some will say it was a glorious madness
The bittern will cry in the wild sky unheard
And Pearce will have gone his way in sadness

Betty may have grown up cherishing her
father's lines
Believing that he lies in shame with the foolish
dead,
Where he fell in some unknown grave in
Ginchy
No honour, just blame, she a child of
circumstance.

Sixteen dead, eleven bullets in each heart
Will be remembered more for their gallant
part,
Fifteen under an Irish sky in Kilmainham
prison yard,
Roger Casement hanged on the gallows in
Pentonville

Tearful mothers, weeping wives, lamenting lovers
Take away lines and letters, parting gifts to them
As brave men impart last farewells and reasons,
Denying futility, claims of the supreme sacrifice

"Your life, James, your beautiful life."
Mary, take these four buttons from my coat,
The only gift Mac Diarmada had left to give
Joseph, my little man, be a priest if you can.

Counting the cost, Mc Donagh was ready to pay
And 'his song floated upwards on the wings of daring'.
Ceannt faced the firing squad after his confession
Content that Ireland had shown she was a nation

Heuston died on a soap box, a calm, fearless youthful face.
Joseph Plunkett went to death husband to his darling Grace
Marriage vows exchanged in the prison chapel, bayonets fixed
And witness words of The Enniskillens chanting prayers.

Beside crucifix carrying priests they walked at dawn

To where a wooden box and sand bags marked
a place,
Hands bound, blindfolded eyes, and stood to
wait
Where writhing bodies fell on blood they
jointly shed.

'Untie my hands, remove the blindfold'.
Wishes of McBride, duty bound, the officer
denied.
A white target square upon his breast, Con
Colbert
Moved it to a higher place upon his heart to
rest.

Thomas Clarke entrusted to his wife a final
message
To let the Irish people know that *with his
fellow-signatories*
*He had struck the first successful blow for
freedom*
*And that the next blow would win through'. He
died happy.*

Hanrahan, Daly and Willie Pearce joined
freely in the fight
And walked to death as brave as any that had
gone before.
Men of vision, Sons of Ireland, faithful and
they fought
And the dream lived on in the conscious heart
of a nation.

ENGRAVED IN A CENTURY

Pearce's; a GAA club in our parish,
Clarkes; the one in Dungannon.
In Belfast college days
I would alight from the trolley bus
at the gates of Casement Park,
passing Connolly House on the way
to Mass at Saint Agnes' Church.

Those names, as common as the Cappagh bus,
nothing special to me, fleetingly mentioned
at my grandmother's knee
or in my father's lapses to the past
on Parnell, Kitty O'Shea and the priests,
or the burning of his conscription letter,
delivered to him by a protestant postman.

School history started with the Tudors,
covered the Reformation,
the Stuarts, the Hanoverians and Victoria
before veering off to Europe
for the Franco-Prussian War,
the occupation of Bosnia and Herzegovina
and the Treaty of Versailles.

The Clarke's played in O'Neill Park
Who was O'Neill? Who was Clarke?
My Godfather was Hugh O'Neill,
our farming neighbour,
whom I watched at work
from my lofty vantage point
upon our march ditch.
A boundary mark between us,
a border that I never crossed.

De Valera's name came and went
There was a man down the road
nick-named De Valera Hughes.
He was tall and slim and wore glasses.
We had our skipping rhymes too,
chanted 'Up De Valera,
The rebels as well.
The Pope is in Heaven.
King Billy's in hell'

A college trip to Dublin in 1966
awakened my interest,
whetted my appetite
to absorb the beauty of a city
steeped in history.
Between visits to art galleries
I toured the dark, dank cells
of Kilmainham prison,
visited the graves at Arbour Hill,
read there the Proclamation
carved on a high wall,
seven signatures;
Clarke, Pearce and Connolly
and others, names new to me.
I saw the bullet-marked pillars
of the GPO in O'Connell Street.
In front of it a crater left by Nelson's Pillar
when it went explosively skyward.

A chain of Irish historical facts
was forming from the links and loops
that came and went in my early days.
A relentless quest followed
as I tried to catch up with the past.

Not only had they cut off the North
They had kept us in the dark.
A history that dare not speak its name
And my parents and family
kept their heads down.
Those passive fears still lingered
that led them to remove the rosary beads,
angled across the holy pictures
when a protestant neighbour called.

I left Belfast in August '69.
A burning city of riots.
A year that marked the birth
Of the so-called 'Troubles'
of the next three decades.
A new generation of republicans emerged.
Names fluttering on roadside banners,
graffitied on roads and walls,
memories engraved on headstones
amongst our family plots.
A decorative cross commemorating a son,
carved with unending Celtic spirals.
Two guns crossed as in friendship,
'Tiocfaidh ár lá' it claims.

The Troubles ended with a 'Peace Process'
but in our parish the reminders remain.
As I stand at my parent's graveside.
I look across at a youthful face
on an embedded ceramic plaque,
an image of a dead hunger striker.
Martin Hurson, a neighbour's son.
I sat beside him on the school bus.
As I move along to the Morris plot,
I pass on the way wreath-bedecked

graves of four young men,
ambushed in Cappagh and Loughgall
by the guns of the SAS and UVF.

One hundred years has passed
and now alongside those of the 1916 dead
we have more commemorative monuments.
Bearing local names, dates and places
Now their lives to us just memories.
Men and women of an unfinished deal.
I can only reecho the words of Pearse;
"They have left us our dead,
think they have foreseen everything,
think they have provided against everything,
but the fools, the fools, fools! ..."

Author's Note: Proclaim The Dream *and* Engraved in a
Century *were poems that resulted from research and
reaction during the 1916 Rising commemoration as part of*
The Risen Word *project, which was supported by the
Ireland 2016 Global and Diaspora Fund and following
attendance at workshops conducted by John McAuliffe.*

AFTER THE LOCKDOWN

A welcome first snowdrop,
to brighten my pathway
and end a year of dark shadows.
Heads dropping downwards
reflecting our sorrows.
New rays of brightness
beckoning forward
to light up our lives
with pure petals of white
in a dim winter sun.

Clear droplets of hope,
yellow beams in their heart
casting a new light
on dead leaves and bracken
with green spikes to follow
from the cold parting soil
as they force through the earth.
A promised new season
in pods of pure beauty.

A SILVER SPOON

James Lynn, the postman, always came to our school every day and we waited eagerly as he gave us letters to take home. That saved him many long journeys on bad roads and wet lanes. One day he had a large parcel on his bicycle carrier. We followed him for our letters but we were also anxious to find out about the parcel he was untying. The Master appeared on the step ad took it from him. That afternoon he came into Mrs. Dolan's room carrying an opened cardboard box. We heard him explain to her that there was one for each pupil.

When he had gone Mrs. Dolan reached into the box and lifted out a small object wrapped in royal blue tissue paper. As she undid the wrapping she told us that it was a special day, there was a new queen being crowned in England and every school pupil in Northern Ireland was to be given a teaspoon with an image of the Queen's on in. It was silver spoon and a piece at the end of the handle was like a shilling. She walked around placing one on each desk, telling us to put it away in our school bag. When she got to the last pupil she still had two left. She thought for a while, put one in handbag and decided to give the extra one to

Audrey Lewis. We all knew that Audrey Lewis was different from us, she was protestant who lived with a family beside the school. She had blonde hair and blue eyes and flesh rimmed national health glasses. There was a sticking plaster across one of the lenses, placed there by the school doctor, to make her lazy eye work.

We had a great story to tell that evening when we got home as we very rarely got any gifts outside of Christmas and even those were of little significance. Our delighted smiles and gushing stories were soon disappearing when she did not get the perceived response to our prized teaspoons. I suggested that we might use one in the sugar bowl but withdrew the suggestion when I saw the shocked look on my mother's face. I suggested another place for it which seemed more acceptable: the tea box.

My sister's teaspoon remained for many years hidden in the press drawer amongst bits of string, puncture repair kit, the elision and sealing wax but mine got well used and tarnished hidden away amongst the tea leaves. Even though it was used at least three times a day no one ever saw the Queen's head, my mother kept that inside her fist when she lifted the leaves to the tea pot.

What was their response to our story of Audrey Lewis getting two teaspoons? My father said, 'she should have been given her the whole lot'.

Author's note: My submission to this retrospective collection reflects the shared thoughts, ideas, support and appreciation of fellow group members in my word journey. It emerged from a time I released the inner feelings of an emigrant, coping and settling into an alien way of life so different to what I had previously experienced on a hill farm within a large family which had instilled in me a love of animals, farming practices, respect for nature and a community spirit.

Steeped in Christian values and Celtic celebrations, cures and superstitions I found reflection on those memories a deep source of inspiration for creativity when expressing my feelings in the written word. Although an artist by profession I sought connections with fellow emigrants in all Irish traditional arts, particularly those who left rural Ireland.

My deep love of nature together with the appreciation of poetry prompted me to develop writing skills that reflect the experiences of that background, my emigrant experience, and the history and heritage of Ireland past and present.

E.M. POWELL

E.M. Powell joined MIW in 2013. Born and raised in Cork city into the family of Michael Collins (the legendary revolutionary and founder of the Irish Free State), she writes medieval mystery and historical thrillers. Her *Stanton & Barling* and *Fifth Knight* novels have been #1 Amazon and Bild bestsellers and have achieved sales of over 500,000 copies worldwide. She has called Manchester her home for almost 25 years, where she and her husband have raised a proud Mancunian/Corkonian hybrid. Find out more at www.empowell.com

MEDIEVAL IRISH WISDOM IN THE NINTH CENTURY TRIADS.

Anyone who loves history will tell you that one of the most enjoyable things to do is to visit actual historical sites. An added bonus of writing historical fiction is that one can do quite a lot of this in the name of research. One of my more recent trips was to the wonderful Dunmore Cave in Co. Kilkenny in Ireland.

Dunmore Cave has been used for refuge and storage for hundreds of years. A Viking massacre here is recorded in the Annals of the Four Masters, a 17th century compilation of earlier Irish chronicles. In 928 Godfrey and the Vikings of Dublin reputedly slaughtered more than 1,000 people here. Archaeological investigations have found the remains of hundreds of people, with many being those of women and children. 10th century coins, beads, and pins have also been found.

I was particularly pleased to see an information board announcing it as 'One of the Three Darkest Places in

Ireland'. No, this wasn't just a cheap marketing ploy by the Irish Office of Public Works. It's a reference to the mention of Dunmore Cave in the Irish Triads. Triads, the arrangement of ideas or sayings in groups of three, are common in ancient Irish and Welsh writing. They are a type of wisdom literature, serving to instruct, enlighten and at times entertain the reader/listener with truths about life.

Trecheng Breth Féne or *The Triads of Ireland* is a collection composed about the ninth century AD by an anonymous author who was most likely a cleric. One might think that the Irish Triad wisdom of over 1,100 years ago would be remote and/or inaccessible. It's quite the opposite. So much of what this unknown writer has left us could have the ink still wet on the paper. I thought I'd share my personal favourites.

Some of the triads are simply a geographical reference, such as to Dunmore Cave above. We have '*The three mountain-passes of Ireland: Baltinglass, the Pass of Limerick, the Pass of Dublin*' and '*The three uneven places of Ireland: Breffny, the Burren, Beare.*' Anyone who has visited the Burren and had a walking boot wedged in a limestone crack would never disagree with this assessment.

Moving on from geography, the writer relates some moral musings:
'*Three rejoicings followed by sorrow: a wooer's, a thief's, a tale-bearer's.*'
'*Three things which justice demands: judgment, measure, conscience.*'
'*Three things which judgment demands: wisdom, penetration, knowledge.*'

Wise indeed, yet quite theoretical. Happily, he gets more specific:
'Three laughing-stocks of the world: an angry man, a jealous man, a niggard.'

Yes, indeed, but closely followed by:
'Three ruins of a tribe: a lying chief, a false judge, a lustful priest.'
'Three ranks that ruin tribes in their falsehood: the falsehood of a king, of a historian, of a judge.'

One has to wonder at this point if the scribe has somehow found a wormhole where he is viewing the 21st century. Leaving his very pertinent observations on human nature, we come to the cleric's Triads that relate to the natural world. These for me have great lyrical beauty.

'Three slender things that best support the world: the slender stream of milk from the cow's dug into the pail, the slender blade of green corn upon the ground, the slender thread over the hand of a skilled woman.'
'Three live ones that put away dead things: a deer shedding its horn, a wood shedding its leaves, cattle shedding their coat.'
'Three cold things that seethe: a well, the sea, new ale.'
'Three sounds of increase: the lowing of a cow in milk, the din of a smithy, the swish of a plough.'
'Three dead things that give evidence on live things: a pair of scales, a bushel, a measuring-rod.'
'Three renovators of the world: the womb of woman, a cow's udder, a smith's moulding-block.'

Beautiful, of course, but this unknown writer didn't simply excel at pastoral imagery. He also has a number of

141

observations of human nature that are on the nail and often hilarious.

'Three rude ones of the world: a youngster mocking an old man, a healthy person mocking an invalid, a wise man mocking a fool.'

'Three ungentlemanly things: interrupting stories, a mischievous game, jesting so as to raise a blush.'

'Three ungentlemanly boasts: I am on your track, I have trampled on you, I have wet you with my dress.' (Note: on this one, I have no idea. I included it because I love it.)

'Three deaths that are better than life: the death of a salmon, the death of a fat pig, the death of a robber.'

'Three silences that are better than speech: silence during instruction, silence during music, silence during preaching.'

'Three speeches that are better than silence: inciting a king to battle, spreading knowledge, praise after reward.'

'Three things that constitute a buffoon: blowing out his cheek, blowing out his satchel, blowing out his belly.'

'Three wealths in barren places: a well in a mountain, fire out of a stone, wealth in the possession of a hard man.'

'Three oaths that do not require fulfilment: the oath of a woman in birth-pangs, the oath of a dead man, the oath of a landless man.'

'Three worst smiles: the smile of a wave, the smile of a lewd woman, the grin of a dog ready to leap.'

The last of the Triads I have included have a particular appeal. They reflect the contemporary world that the writer lived in, such as this one about Irish appearance:

'Three lawful handbreadths: a handbreadth between shoes and hose, a handbreadth between ear and hair, a handbreadth between the fringe of the tunic and the knee.'

142

The world of work is here, too.

'Three things that constitute a comb-maker: racing a hound in contending for a bone; straightening a ram's horn by his breath, without fire; chanting upon a dunghill so that all antlers and bones and horns that are below come to the top.'

'Three things that constitute a carpenter: joining together without calculating, without warping; agility with the compass; a well-measured stroke.'

'Three things that constitute a physician: a complete cure, leaving no blemish behind, a painless examination.'

'Three things that constitute a harper: a tune to make you cry, a tune to make you laugh, a tune to put you to sleep.'

And as it's Ireland, we have views on hospitality. First, things the writer isn't happy with:

'Three unfortunate things for a man: a scant drink of water, thirst in an ale-house, a narrow seat upon a field.'

'The three worst welcomes: a handicraft in the same house with the inmates, scalding water upon the feet, salt food without a drink.'

'Three preparations of a bad man's house: strife before you, complaining to you, his hound taking hold of you.'

'Three sorrowful ones of an alehouse: the man who gives the feast, the man to whom it is given, the man who drinks without being satiated.'

Counterbalanced with what he approves of:

'Three preparations of a good man's house: ale, a bath, a large fire.'

'Three entertainers of a gathering: a jester, a juggler, a lap-dog.'

'Three accomplishments of Ireland: a witty stave, a tune on the harp, shaving a face.'

'Three fewnesses that are better than plenty: a fewness of fine words, a fewness of cows in grass, a fewness of friends around good ale.'

But I think he must be back at that wormhole, looking over my shoulder. For, lastly, we have:

'Three glories of speech: steadiness, wisdom, brevity.'

I'll accept that 1,100-year-old advice: brevity it is. Slán!

Author's note: My third Fifth Knight *medieval thriller,* The Lord of Ireland, *was inspired by an audience member at a MIW-hosted book launch held at the Irish World Heritage Centre in 2013. They asked if I would ever write a novel of Medieval Ireland. I said no, the research would be too hard. But the idea was planted!*

So I did—and indeed it was hard. But it was also glorious to mine just some of Ireland's ancient history and find wonders like the wisdom of the Triads.

And I have fellow Manchester Irish Writer Kevin McMahon to thank for naming a character in The Lord of Ireland. *The character is a huge, battle-axe wielding Irish warrior. I gave Kevin ridiculous parameters: 'I want to give my character a single Irish name that describes him. I also need to avoid the following letters that would start his name, as it can look clumsy on the page when people have the same one. So, to avoid: B, C, D, E, J (I know that's out anyway in the Irish alphabet, along with K, Q, V, W, X, Y, Z, if memory serves me correctly), G, H, L, N, O, P, R (but might get away with this one), T.'*

Despite my ridiculous parameters, Kevin came back with Uinseann, which means 'victor'. A wonderful and wise choice, and one example among so many from the inspiring and supportive Manchester Irish Writers.

MARION RILEY

Marion was born in Limerick city, emigrating to Manchester as a young teenager. She has lived and worked in Spain, Sardinia, France and Switzerland, She has been a winner and runner-up in several writing competitions run by *Ireland's Own* magazine, and has seen several short stories published in that periodical. Marion edited her mother's memoir, *From Kerry Child to Limerick Lady*, and has had monologues performed at the Library Theatre, Manchester. She had enjoyed numerous successes in poetry competitions, and has even written a Spanish memoir, and articles for a newspaper in Madrid. Now Marion is trying to slow life down by focusing on one idea at a time.

MY FRIEND'S DONEGAL HOSPITALITY

I remember, oh how I remember as if it was only yesterday, the Manchester Irish Dance Halls in the late 50's and early 60's. Just over from Limerick, my sense of not belonging and homesickness was relieved by the friendship of a second-generation Irish girl and her sisters whose mother and father hailed from Donegal.

They lived in Moss Side but my parents had no idea of this district's rough reputation. I even walked through the streets on a New Year's Eve alone, having lost Theresa. But not once was I accosted, just a cheerful Happy New Year from friendly revellers as they passed me by.

Theresa's parents' hospitality was amazing. Their home always open to their children's teenage friends. Not only did they cook us dinners and breakfasts but there was always sandwiches, cold meats and hard boiled eggs left out when we returned. starving hungry, from a dance.

They allowed us to be the giggly, lively, teenagers that we were. Sometimes boys called to go with us to the dances. They weren't boyfriends, just family friends and before we got ready, we'd all jump up and down on the beds, playfight with pillows, tease each other unmercifully. We were so innocent and so free.

For us girls, the highlight of the weekends was the actual getting ready for the dances, though often anticipation proved better than participation. How we struggled with the false eyelash glue, often getting it in our eyes. We backcombed our hair until birds could have built their nests in it. And oh those petticoats beneath the dresses! We often wore more than one, all flouncy and bouncy. We put nylon stockings down our bras to make us look shapelier, and even foam-filled pads. One night while dancing a jive, my pad fell on to the floor, but I just kicked it away in a nonchalant fashion and carried on dancing, not caring that my silhouette was lobsided.

Friday was Sharrocks night, followed by Saturdays at the Astoria. Then on the dot of 3pm we were back at Sharrocks again on Sunday afternoons.

The band played dances in threes. Three Quick Steps which could be rock n roll too. Then there was usually a waltz followed by a so-called Foxtrot. I say so called, because I doubt any of us knew how to do a true Foxtrot or indeed a Quick Step or Viennese Waltz. We just wanted to move our bodies to the rhythm of the music and show off our fancy underskirts as we twirled around the floor. And then after an hour or so came The Siege of Ennis or The Walls of

Limerick. This was a chance to get to meet all the different young men as we swung madly around, often ending in a flurry of flouncy skirts entwined with a young man on the floor.

Those were the days of the mighty Showbands, especially during Lent when dances weren't allowed in Ireland. The Premier Aces, Blue Aces, The Royal Showband, Royal Blues, Clipper Carltons, The Vanguard 6 and Big Tom and the Mainliners to name just a few.

I did occasionally go to an English hall, where if my memory serves me right, alcohol was served, but nothing compared to the Irish dances. For like most young emigrants I needed the company of Irish boys and girls who shared the same sense of humour and fun. English boys of my own age seemed so sophisticated. With the Irish lads one could have a laugh, or as they say nowadays, enjoy the craic.

And then the Blarney opened in Cheetham Hill followed by the Assembly Rooms, so I didn't need to be going off to the other side of Manchester as I lived nearby. But often the lads who walked me home did live on the other side of the city. They had to walk back through Manchester city and suburbs and for what? If lucky a kiss or two and a promise to meet the following week. Oh, we were heartless, us girls, in those days!

I sometimes went to the Astoria (later called The Carousel) with my friend after she met the love of her life. The happy couple always included me, and I vividly remember a photographer taking my picture with his monkey perched on my head fiddling with my bird's nest.

Theresa sadly died in her early sixties and so I can't reminisce with her about those days when we danced and sang. Those days we thought would never end, when we felt immortal.

But I'll never forget her and her parents' kindness in making me, a young naïve emigrant, feel so much at home.

Author's note: A nostalgic piece focusing on the ways in which the older generation helped young emigrants like me to feel less isolated in 1950s Manchester.

ANNETTE SILLS

Annette was born in Wigan, Lancashire to parents from Co. Mayo, Ireland. Her short stories have been longlisted and shortlisted in a number of competitions including The Fish Short Story Prize, *Books Ireland* Magazine, *The Telegraph* Short Story Club. Her first two novels were published by Poolbeg Press in Dublin. She is currently writing a third. Annette's stories are set in the Manchester Irish diaspora. She currently lives in Chorlton, Manchester with her husband and two children.

THE HISTORY MAN

He always visited the week before Christmas. He turned up at six on the dot and never left later than ten. He drank no more than two neat nips of Powers whisky and ate a Red Leicester cheese sandwich made with my mother's home-made soda bread. Without fail my sisters and I were presented with a carrier bag filled with joy: Love Hearts, Cola bottles, various flavoured bon bons and large bars of Cadbury's Fruit and Nut. We never had the heart to tell him we disliked nuts but the minute he'd gone we clawed at the silver wrappers and nibbled the chocolate off like three desperate mice.

He looked out of place in our cramped front room with its weary floral three piece, three bar gas fire, and chipped ornamental Irish cottages. The deep velvet and dark oak of The Garrick or Trafford Conservative Club would have suited him better. A short compact man, he had an unruly hedge of hair well in his seventies that was probably held down by a battalion of barbers on a regular basis and tamed and brylcreemed to perfection. In his later years he wore tweed and corduroy and cashmere pullovers in autumn shades and aftershave with a hint of apple. I was once sent into throes of ecstasy by a well-cut double- breasted grey pin striped suit, a lavender silk tie and gold cufflinks in the shape of a military crest. Known as Breaffy Jim, he was my father's uncle and he lived at the other end of the world in North Manchester where he worked as a foreman on a building site. Presumably there was another Jim in the family somewhere in Ireland who did not live in Breaffy, but no one seemed to know whom.

We were given a couple of hours with him before bedtime, and he would swing one of us on to his knee while the other two sat cross legged at his feet gazing at their reflection in his Italian leather shoes. There were some jokes but he mainly told us stories, conjured up from every nook and cranny of history, dusted off and brought to life with humour, suspense and an array of funny voices. Under his spell I was a time traveller, transported out of our dreary Levenshulme terrace to other worlds; the Easter Rising, both world wars, Tudor times and The Civil Rights Movement. His accent was anglicised, with very little of my father's harsh Mayo brogue, his voice soft and fluid, like water trickling over stones, As we got older the sweets were replaced by books, glossy illustrated hardbacks with one or two still retaining a library stamp on the back page. I'd sneak them into my room away from my sisters who were far more interested in their Jackie annuals at that point anyway. I was devastated when he didn't return after the argument. Christmas was never the same again. Some of the glitter and sparkle had gone from it.

Mother and Breaffy Jim did not get on. Wide of hip and sharp of tongue, she was a pragmatic woman from County Clare who kept a picture of a young De Valera in full military uniform hanging above the fireplace next to the

151

Sacred Heart. Jim was deferential in her presence but distant. She sniffed at his stories and his 'fancy ways' and objected to cleaning up the nuts off her carpet after his visits. But I felt very drawn to him though I could not articulate why until later. "He's like me", I used to tell myself. "He's just like me." I was thirteen at the time of his last visit, struggling to make sense of the world and looking for my place in it. I was in bed with my head stuck in his latest offering, an illustrated history of the Black Panther Movement, when I heard raised voices in the living room followed by the front door slamming. I jumped out of bed and pulled back the nets to see his red Vauxhall Victor bouncing down the cobbles.

I could hear my parents arguing in the kitchen, so I crept downstairs, sat down halfway and listened. My father sounded very upset.

"For Christ's sake, Tess. Why did you have to tell him?"

"He had a right to know."

"You should have left well alone."

"He had a right to know his brother is dying. How was I to know he'd want to go back? The cheek of him. After all these years. Sure he never even went back for your Mammy or Daddy's funeral."

I strained to hear what my father said next over the scream of the kettle.

"Never forgave them for giving my father the home place. He worked the farm for five years when Da was in America then he was turfed out on the street when he came back and married my mother. And purely because Da was the first born. I wouldn't mind but they all said Jim was by far the better farmer. He cleared his throat. "But everyone knows that is the reason he isn't welcome. Tis only an excuse."

"What he did was disgusting. It brought shame on to your family."

"Ah, give over woman. You're as bad as the bigots over there. He wasn't the only one. There were plenty more did what he did."

"It does not make it right. Your mother and father had to live with it for years afterwards. People talking behind their backs and making snide comments."

I heard the scrape of a chair and footsteps. "I'm not listening to any more of this shite. I'm going to bed. People – you included, need to cop on and move with the times. The past is the past. There's many did far worse and Jim doesn't deserve to be treated like a leper for the rest of his days."

At the creak of the door handle I scampered up the stairs and slid into bed. I lay awake the whole of that night going over and over what I'd just heard, thoughts racing around my head like a greyhound on a track. I was filled with terror and self-loathing and I tossed and turned until dawn, fearful for the life ahead of me.

Breaffy Jim was never spoken about in our house again, but my father continued to meet with him. He suffered a stroke in later life and went into a home where he lingered until his death at the age of ninety-four in 1984. My father informed me when I was home from Oxford for the weekend. Jim's stories and books had left their mark on me.

I had just completed a BA in Modern History at Trinity College and was about to embark on a Masters, for which I'd been awarded a scholarship.

My sister Clare was pregnant with the family's first grandchild at the time and on the Saturday morning I gave her and Mother a lift into town to shop for baby gear. Mother was puce-faced and puffed with the heat and all the extra weight she'd piled on over the years and I secretly wondered if she was actually about to self-combust at the prospect of the new arrival. She'd talked of nothing else in wearing sentimental tones since I got there the previous evening and Clare and I were stifling laughter as she threw a number of ridiculous names at us from the back seat.

"I don't think Claire's keen on Brian or Deirdre, Mother," I said as my sister snorted in the passenger seat.

"It's about time you were thinking about settling down and having children of your own," she replied in that barbed tone she had that used to cut me to the core as a boy.

I said nothing but Claire stepped in.

"Don't be daft, Mum. He's but a wee lamb." She threw me a warm smile and patted the Morrissey quiff I sculpted every morning that attracted so many curious looks in the college quads. "He can't possibly be a Daddy with a barnet like this."

Mother sniffed. "Well, he can't spend all his life doing his hair or reading books either."

By the time I got back, Dad's flushed face indicated that he'd been drinking, which was unusual as he wasn't a daytime tippler. He was sitting in the back yard that could no longer be called that as it had recently acquired a small lawn, flower beds and two aluminium garden chairs. It was a glorious June day with cobalt blue skies and a soothing breeze that quivered through Dad's carefully tended carnations and roses. I sat down next to him, helped myself to a can from the cooler box by his side and stretched out my legs. In my five whole doc martins, black Levi's and black Smiths T shirt, I felt like a streak of charcoal slicing through a floral landscape.

Dad took hold of a carrier bag hanging from the side of the chair and put it on his knee, his hands trembling slightly. "Do you remember my uncle that used to come and visit when ye were small?"

"Of course," I nodded, my stomach churning slightly," Breaffy Jim. I remember him well."

"He passed away in the home a couple of weeks ago."

"Yeah? Sorry to hear that."

He shook his head and laughed. "The poor fella was an awful handful at the end. Completely gone, telling the nurses to kiss his hole in Irish and re-enacting scenes from the war. He'd yell military orders at the top of his voice when they were all sitting down for tea and he'd wake in the night drenched in sweat, shaking and screaming. God love him. The nurses said a lot of the veterans are the same."

"Veterans?" I threw him a blank look and he reached into the plastic bag.

"Breaffy Jim was in the Great War, son. He fought at the Somme with The Dublin Fusiliers." The silvery voice, the gold cufflinks with the military crest, it all came back to me. I shook my head slowly.

"All those stories.... he never once mentioned it."

"He was told not to. Your mother, well not just her but a lot of Irish people, nationalists, were ashamed when one of their own joined the British Army back then. They were seen as traitors and they didn't like to talk about it. Many soldiers never returned home. They weren't welcome and they were shunned and denied work." He hung his head. "Your mother didn't want any of you to know about Jim."

I thought back to the night of the argument and the conversation between my parents in the kitchen and the true meaning of what I heard dawned on me. I felt a sharp pang for the confused boy I was back then and my innocent misinterpretation. I lost something that night. I never forgot my parents' words and I carried them with me throughout my turbulent teenage years.

Dad pulled a palm-sized red velvet box the out of the carrier bag and handed it to me. "Jim left you this."

I opened the box. Inside was a medal. I took it out, turned it over in my hand and read the simple inscription. "For War Service. James Corley. Royal Dublin Fusiliers."

"He was very proud of his great nephew. He always asked after you when I wheeled him round the gardens of the home. 'How's The History Man doing?' he'd say in his lucid moments. His eyes always lit up whenever your name was mentioned." He looked at me shyly then nodded down

156

at the medal. "Jim's friend Ralph gave it to me in the club after the funeral. He and Jim were very close, friends for over fifty years. I don't think he stopped crying the whole of the service. He visited him every day in the home. He said Jim wanted you to have it."

I looked up and locked eyes with my father, startled by the blue of the sky reflected there. Then I realised he was trying to tell me he knew. He knew the secret I had kept locked away from him since I was twelve years old for fear of rejection and exile.

I was suddenly filled with love for him, and I clasped my fingers around the medal, the silver cooling my sweating palm. As I pulled my gaze away it rested on a small swallowtail hovering on the back of his chair. I watched as it lifted above his shoulder, hovered, then opened its wings and soared.

Author's note: The History Man *was inspired by a series of workshops with Manchester Irish Writers centred around the anniversary of The Easter Rising of 1916. The writings we studied and subsequent discussions triggered memories of my great uncle Jimmy, a Mayo man who left Ireland and fought for the British Army in World War II.* The History Man *is loosely based on him.*

PATRICK SLEVIN

Patrick joined the Manchester Irish Writers in 2016. His poems have been published in *Poetry Ireland Review, New Isles Press, The Cormorant, Skylight 47, The Poets' Republic, Manchester Review, The Interpreter's House, Drawn to the Light, The Blue Nib, The High Window, The Cabinet of Heed, Bangor Literary Journal, Ink, Sweat and Tears, Degenerate Literature* amongst others, and he has been featured on RTE's Poem of the Day as well as appearing in the anthologies *Something About Home* and *The Best of the Cormorant.*

WORK PASSES

I'd call them souvenirs. It's not hoarding.
Not when you've the set. The full set (I think).
Sellotape – bruised with age – holds the box
together.
They're here. Inside. Unblemished. Clinging
on
to lives that didn't stick. Vague markers
lining all roads
to now. Temporary
paper affairs. Sliding, writing
in polythene holds. Shot against bland
backdrops
in colour not so modern now. Original sins
shading the soul slowly
a little darker. A day here. Weeks there.
Sometimes
months. Eyes fixed beyond
the lens in seasons
already revolving doors as nothing changed

but everything in silent fragile calm.

First published in The Cabinet of Heed.

SETTLING THINGS

…and there were stray ones,
and twos, and threes – they had to be balanced
as well. If pressed I've have guessed
about sixty – from glances
at plastic bags, from memories
of him gasping – just get me the four – a reflex
that made everything alright.
Maybe it cleared up
the inhaler that rouletted to silence
in the glass ashtray he'd kept – sometimes
it's quieter to leave things in full view
so a question doesn't appear.
That's how everyone knew
your name and number were scrawled
on the envelope
in the dust. Visible now
in its absence – like the last sip –
a thumb's width headlining
the top of the glass, on the only table
by that only chair
in front of the single bed, surrounded
by a wall of one-hundred and eighteen cans
and you, you'd have thrown them away.

First published in Bangor Literary Review.

CARBOOT

Every scratch from every needle
is hidden inside these sleeves –
the scars off inadvertent drops
from when a certain personal hit
was needed – carried around
in square bags worn as badges
accumulated on Saturdays
browsing Eastern Bloc, Decoy,
Golden Disc, Piccadilly –
dancing footsteps with fingers
along the tops of boxes,
the same as he does now
before he stops and, glancing –
not part of the crowd
pressing for phones, holding on
to seized-up watches, uninterested
in unread biographies – asks
as if it's nothing, for me
to put a price on it all.

First published in Ink, Sweat and Tears

SNAPSHOT

The youngest points at 'The Essential Neruda'
leant against a one Euro bottle of Holy Water
and some other more essential essentials. She
thinks it's your cousin
with his forearm across the top of his head,
and

is that a magpie? I've never looked that close
but it's true there's a resemblance.

160

I explain. All she asks is – *what country? Is he dead?*
With her it's always nothing but death.

The upshot is we're going to Chile.
It's been decided – so I can visit his grave
and she can stay in hotel. She's always wanted to.
They have swimming pools and water slides.

Later, you remember Kefalonia. That night
we took a picture of the taxi-driver.
A perfect double for your cousin you thought.
It might still be loose in the back of an album.

First published in The Manchester Review

MOSS

Scraping into the silence of another empty afternoon,
the dogwalkers, who never stops, hovers, explores,
runs through power washes. That unknown neighbour
leans on the fence, weighs up, once overs the maze
of Accrington brick, confirms – it's nothing but residue
after this dry spell and reckons on the amount
of silver sand need. Together we lose ourselves
around possibilities – thin chisel? thick nail?
Brush through
pound shops that might or might not be gone

now the pole's skin has loosened in the grip of
seasons
unused beneath patio rain. Still, I carry on.
Even you
admit this could be therapeutic – all this
tapping, a bit
hypnotic and longer for more of the action
with tea
at the door. I explain, perhaps it's my previous
in data-entry? Or the years lost to Tetris? Both
now
enough of a distance to gaze into. Maybe
though
sometimes, occasionally, you just need
something,
like Everest, because it's there, so I hear.
Whatever
the build-up shifts, lifts – effortlessly if you
listen, slowly
out from the edges, somewhere along those
lines.

First published in The Manchester Review.

THE WAY BACK

They didn't expect me to lead the log flume.
To make them stay on for another pirate ship.
To lean back on the helter skelter
and raise my hands in victory. Later,

when they asked me in the car, I told them.
We never went to fairs. The older ones
might have gone but when I came along
that was done. I turned up a song of theirs

162

to fill the silence that couldn't be filled.
Then I told them. But I went to fairs, later,
on my own. And I went on all the rides,
hunting shadows in the flashing lights

in those black clothed teenage years
pretending to be with that group to all
the watching eyes. Silent. Desperate to go
faster.
Not screaming. Never. Not until today.

First published in The Manchester Review

SELFIE MODE

They've set up an account
on a tablet – his prescription, his medicine –
with no friends or family or photographs,
only a link to his home parish
and a password that's been saved
and written down with instructions – who to
call
in case. He's been warned
not to mess with the volume, just to jab
that deliberate finger and hold on
at arms-length at ten any day
and he'll be on the front-row
sixty years back across the sea
five-hundred miles to the west
wishing they'd show more of the empty pews
he struggles to fill as they float
to the door at the end, while he waits, prays
for some glimpse of life he can place
going past for exercise on the Mall.

Afterwards – only on Sundays –
he calls his last sister down south
to explain the priest made the sign of the cross
with his left-hand again. They can't
understand why he does that.

First published in The Blue Nib.

POSSIBLY VENICE

The dark shirt camouflages the camera.
Off-hand, his watch arm reaches out

two or three war-calloused fingers.
She wraps her softened mill-girl's palm

around them, behind the elbow
up, almost backwards. From under the sunhat

her eyes pierce to their right, perhaps
to a canal. He stares dead on

down the lens, almost breaking
into a grin. In tandem

their inside shoes tread flat. On the outside
they are caught in the motions

of this eternal step, casting
a conjoined shadow on the flags

sauntering towards the unknown
photographer – no doubt dripping

in patter, a ticket book ready, bent at the knees

focusing, choreographing

these chances before the stairs
sweep the outline

of a half-visible building. Way back
a spire recedes

into the off-sepia sky. The clockface,
too distant to be anything

but blank, hovers over their shoulders.
Possibly it's Venice.

Always it's always. Always.

First published in The Blue Nib

NIGHT BOAT

The seats haven't changed
since last year. Bodies wash up
marooned by the news.
Someone's been at the volume.

A girl smiles – they were sat there.
Football shirts run free
down the wrong walkway, with pints,
bend their knees, wait for sea legs

then double-back. Everyone watches
the children no-one's watching.
A couple stroll around the shop
for the third time, pick up the same toy,

it makes no difference
the exchange is closed.
Dawn pushes in, pale with Dublin.
Laughter drifts through the swing doors.

First published in Poetry Ireland Review.

CHRISTMAS 1978

We didn't ask him to play dead. His record
was three days.
But we kicked each other over like he'd told
us then cleared the battlefield.
We spied his advance, inch by inch, the big
shoe dragging,
polished beneath a sharp crease. False teeth
gritted
above the perfect Windsor, hair blown wild
over no-man's land.
To accordion songs he tapped along, haunted
by an absent quickstep,
smiling through the frostbite that kept his
counting steady at thirteen.

Machine gun laughter rattled out from under
that German tree,
thick glasses misted as brandy smoke rose-up
from the pudding trench.
Wincing with every crunch of spoon of
Vienetta on best plates
he closes his eyes for desert, it was said he
could sleep anywhere.

A sixty-year old shout stopped the house but
he didn't see us at all.

Then he said his foot was cold, and everyone
laughed, and I
laughed with the adults. It was warm in the
Christmas ceasefire
playing Subbuteo in the lounge.

First published in The Interpreter's House.

THE LIGHT FROM HERE

Tonight, up here – because the light's stayed
longer –
we fly kites. They weave and waltz
and orbit. Tiny diamond trails shadow dance
each jewel – the same as moons. We feel the
pull
between stone walls inside the fields
on still grass. Stars slide out
unnoticed, out of the blue so dark
it's settled – the sky's always been like this.

Of course, I'm left to reel them in – the kites.
Slowly. One by one. To make sure
they're not tangled. In the clear it's me
and just the stars. I see things.
Draw lines out there of old shapes.
Trace names into the nothing
scattered across night's acres – remains that
shone
and died, unconcerned, leaving space

for unseen worlds to track tomorrow's suns.
Years – millions of years from now –
maybe someone (or thing) up there
might in a moment

treading water on a dark rock
gaze out to their alien sky alone and –
unknown
to them – catch the light that slipped through
here
tonight, out of our fading star.

First published in The Cormorant.

REUNION

What I remember is the camera
we borrowed. How
we wound the film on
instead of reeling it in
exposing the negatives
to too much light.
We could have waited.
Found someone
who understood the workings
but in the rush
ended up with nothing.
In this empty moment
with the eyes you've just told me I still have
I squint through that viewfinder
at those undeveloped pictures.
The distance is right.
The image is perfect.

First published in Drawn to the Light Press

IN THE BIG HOUSE

The reason you don't see any smiles
is that they didn't have any teeth,
not past thirty – that's when
portraits were done, generally,
the volunteer volunteers. Check,
there are over a hundred
dotted around these walls
and not one smile in all this
splendour. Of course
they never bathed either,
despite their finery, maybe
once a year, no more. And these
remember, were in the big house,
not our people, who never sat
at any table.

First published in The Poet's Republic

THE LAST HOUSE

She'll tell Tommy about the outside lamp
tomorrow,
when she sees him. If she sees him. I imagine
she's just as wrong-footed by this absolute
dark
that's come in unnoticed with a late chill
on the heels of the early heatwave, but
while I'm establishing the exact whereabouts
of the car – adjusting, becoming accustomed –
she's off
on the unsteady gallop of her good and bad
legs

with the stick she uses as a crutch, pointing
with the latest last cigarette (still not believing
I've gone electric) into the moonless, starless
pitch
where the hills play – day in, day out – and
names them, shames them who've left, one by
one
precisely – Lenehan, Duffy, Cawley,
McGing…
mumbling clearly – 'There was great company
in those lights where the village used to
stretch'.

First published in Skylight 47

LAST THING

Loose stones echo. Walls
bed down at the fields' seams.
That skull of a ruin grins.
Specks of light blossom
into smudges
we put names on,
give some shape to, as if
this townland's an asterism.
Pressed back, the sky
dribbles stars
then overflows. Headlamps
scything a road
out of pure darkness
are disappeared.
Almost transparent – moths
rush in circles like lost souls.

First published in The Cormorant.

Author's note: Writers write. Alone. The very idea of being a writer (can there be any other idea?) is to embrace being alone and not to be afraid of the blank page. But there are times when the writer needs a refuge. Somewhere they can be. Where they can talk about writing. The process. A place, like the space we hover in after reverse before first, (not writing but crucially not not-writing) where you can meet fellow travellers. For reaction to writing. For ideas. For inspiration on the journey to your own voice. Manchester Irish Writers is that space for me. Where I reach out to others trying to articulate the chaos that is life. Where I can sit with writers and talk. See a different viewpoint. The smallest comment can have the biggest impact. The biggest comment can have none. But nonetheless, it doesn't matter. It is a place where friends meet and discuss the passion that drives us.

CAROLINE WELDON

Caroline was born in Manchester to Irish parents and has been a member of the Manchester Irish Writers since April 2019. Her initial interest was writing prose – short stories and memoir type pieces based on Irish social history. The breadth of knowledge, experience, skill set and accomplishments within the group, provide Caroline, as a relative newcomer, with a treasure trove to draw on, which has enabled her to develop her writing and to diversify into other areas such as poetry.

RHYTHMIC FOOTSTEPS

Methodical placement of footsteps,
Rhythmic comfort,
Wind buffeting yet guiding.
Tracing the hypnotic bay curve,
Mountain collar surround,
Giving way to light filled expanse.
Cold, wet, firm,
Reassuring sand grains,
A golden layer,
On the sole.

Distant lilting high jinks,
A dash of madness,
Galloping into clear sparkling waters.
Aonbarr and Manannán Mac Lir.
Wave sweeping their foam laced domain.
Blue tinged freckled skin,
Purple edged lips,
Laughing through chattering teeth.

Methodical placement of footsteps,

Soothing ebb and flow,
Dragging its bounty.
Shell and creature fragments,
Entangled in a seaweed mesh.
Gentle hushing back and forth,
Lulling and calming
On the soul.

Author's note; Postscript by Seamus Heaney, was the inspiration for this poem, following a MIW meeting regarding his work. It is based on my family holidays in Donegal, with links to Irish mythology – Manannán Mac Lir (an Irish sea God) and his horse Aonbarr.

THE LAST TINGES

The solid black lie of the land,
The last ochreous tinges,
Fade upwards to silvered blue.

Pencil stroke ragged branches,
Pierce the horizon of colours,
As upturned roots seek soil.

Few remaining wisps of cloud,
Weightless, gentle gliding,
Yield to night sky stillness.

An luminous speck multiplies,
The silvered blue stretches and deepens,
Tinges diminish on the line muted black.

Author's note: The wonder of nature and a view from a window of a winter sunset prompted this poem, a painting in words.

MORNING MOON

Undulating verdant shades,
Slate blue trimming,
Interlaced blush white.
Morning moon peers,
Behind partial grey veil.

Solitary snowdrop,
Daring daffodil shoot,
Splits stubborn grass tufts.
Distant tree cluster,
Huddled in a russet hue.

A raven flies through stillness,
Pheasant struts palette plumage.
Captured hare glimpse,
Dark darting shapes,
Against the lush texture.

Author's note: This piece continues the view from a window theme.

NATURE'S MATINEE

Tattered, torn, shaken,
Battle scarred periphery,
Rooted core standing firm.
Gushes softening to sigh,
Quake reduced to tremble.

Whisper, strengthening whirr,
Slight shiver towards sway,
Struggle reviving,
Blustering crescendo,

Whips through reaching fingers,

Patchwork degrees of grey,
Contain nature's matinee,
Under a blanketed dome.

Author's note: The calm of the morning moon replaced by a stormy afternoon.

BULLETS AND BUS TICKETS

Passion, patriotism, freedom,
A scholar of Irish history.
Embedded tales of rebellion,
Inciting my desire,
For justice and autonomy.

Self-belief and youthful swagger,
Familiar with ditch and hillock,
Hidden underground caves.
Operating under the radar,
Making our presence felt.

Violence upped on both sides,
Fear and adrenaline pumping,
Towards our end goal.
This is our time!
Truce.

Whispers of a treaty,
First seeds of qualm,
A perfidious act.
Disbelief and rage!
A split.

Oneness riddled,
Suspicion and division,
Loyalty switches to treachery.
How did my brother in arms
Become the enemy within?

Comrades who fought by my side,
Now incarcerate
My betrayal and despair.
Prison release bittersweet,
Under a new regime.

Beguiling America beckons.
My alienated troop,
Treading in ancestors' footsteps.
A new world – New York –
My loss has a glimmer of hope.

Rawness of battle,
State of high alert,
Exchanged for daily routine,
Issuing bus tickets not bullets,
Leading to partial contentment.

Self-doubt and ageing acceptance,
Yearning for my home ever-.present
Return to the family farm,
Marriage and raising children,
Fading echoes of turbulent times.

Eventual recognition,
Granted a military pension.
Awarded a commemorative medal/
An independent Ireland,
Though not the young scholar's vision

Author's note: This piece is based on, my maternal Grandfather's experience of the Irish War of Independence and the Civil War.

STACK OF RIFLES

Rifles stacked in the corner,
Unwanted visitors.
Low voices,
The odd volley of laughter,
Hungry, tired, still guarded.

Crowded kitchen,
Men on the run.
Hint of a smile, nod of recognition,
From others an unknowing glance.
Careless flicking of ash onto the stone floor.

Rhythmic clanking of the spoon,
Grandmother making tea.
Mammy's face betraying, smooth slicing,
The sway and slash of the scythe,
Casting Daddy a lone shadow in the fields.

A comment about the treaty.
Mammy stills then turns,
Bread knife remaining in hand.
Grandmother with a taut reply.
Ensuing silence.

Ticking clock absorbs the charged quiet,
Willing these men to go,
After eating their fill,
Moving in an orderly fashion,

One by one collecting their rifles.

All sound extinguished,
Exiting the property,
Under cover of darkness.
The old house and its occupants
Breathing a collective sigh of relief.

Author's note: This poem is based on my paternal Grandfather's recollection from boyhood of an event in the Civil War.

SILENCING SILVER

The head tilted and neck at an awkward angle was necessary, to protect her eyes from the cutting, fine snow falling at a rapid rate. For a fleeting moment, she worried that she must look an odd sight to the others sharing her stretch of pavement. However, in her middle age she was beyond obsessing about appearance.

The soft pad of the worn-out trainers and swish of her sleeves brushing past her sides, went some way to giving her the reassurance which she craved today. The determined quick paced strides made her feel energised and youthful as she passed an elderly couple, making careful, small, trepid movements. That was until the ache just below her left knee made a re-appearance.

With a backward glance, smugness turned to envy, observing the gentle guiding arm and caring gestures.

The doppler effect of each passing car had a strange comfort, interrupting her thoughts in a good way. She mused over methods to keep busy as a distraction. She knew some acquaintances who were constantly on the go and wondered was this a technique, so they didn't have to dwell on negative thoughts, but she wasn't one of these people. Regardless of how she occupied her time, the raw nagging doubts and over analysing would creep back.

'We are appealing for new witnesses to come forward. No matter how small or insignificant you think the information is...'

She re-played today's news bulletin over and over in her head.

She had seen it – the argument, the pushing that developed into slaps and thrown punches. Making her way onto the deck to clear her head, she heard raised voices, dismissing it as a couple of boyos who had over-indulged in the bar. As she drew nearer the voices, the words, the tone and volume made her suddenly halt. She tried to place the accents – one had a definite west of Ireland lilt, the other was more difficult – English – southern she thought. Unsure what to do, she remained in the shadows, holding her breath, the briny, tangy air still filling her nostrils. The wind chill and sea spray lashed against her raw skin as she tried to prevent her clothes flapping around her, staying as stiff as a board. She closed her eyes and wished she could close her ears, focussing on the slash of the waves against the boat, the thrashing flag and rope clanging against the pole.

And then silence... The wind had dropped and she no longer heard the harsh words, the connection of fist against jaw, the scuffle and groans, the staggering of feet to gain the upper hand. Relieved she batted her eyes open, sighing out all of her breath. Only to see the flash of the blade removed from the chest, the look of bewilderment as the victim's gaze dropped to see the trickle of crimson trailing along his checked jacket. His body followed the gaze and slumped down against the rails. The lifting and pushing executed in one smooth movement. She was surprised that the splash wasn't very loud, but that final sound would permeate her thoughts and dreams for years to come.

The urgency to flee filled her chest, until it felt like it was racing up her throat and out of her mouth, but she knew she would have stay silent and motionless. The casual fling of the knife flickering through the air and tossing of a half-finished cigarette, almost made her question what had occurred. Hoping her ordeal was at an end, she listened as the footsteps started to move away and the cumbersome door to the inside warmth shut with a heavy thud. For the second time she let out a quivering sigh. She scrambled to look overboard but all that was visible was the white trimmed black swell. In desperation she threw the lifebuoy ring into the vast darkness. Her body released from its stillness began to tremble violently as she sank to the cold, hard deck, her mind whirring around in a state of confusion.

Still shaky but conscience fuelled, she pushed herself to standing, marched up to and yanked the deck door open. In her rush she misjudged the high step and lost her footing – a hand shot out to support her arm.

A charming smile, 'Mind how you go,' should have reassured her. Thank you died on her lips as she stared into the eyes of the southern accent. 'It's a cold night for a stroll on deck. Don't suppose there's many venturing outside. Not much to see or to be telling anyone,' The glint in his cold blue eyes reminded her of the flash of the flickering blade.

Muttering with a half-smile she regained her balance and began to walk away, feigning an unhurried manner. His second generation attempt at an Irish accent, followed her down the corridor, 'And you on your way back from visiting the boyfriend down the country.'

Cursing herself for wearing the oversized Galway jersey, she found the Ladies. After locking herself in a cubicle, she remained there in a stupor unable to carry out her plan. She waited until she was sure, she would be one of the last to disembark. As she walked quickly through the empty lounge towards the stairs – she tried to persuade herself – there's still time to raise the alarm. She would do it once she was safely off the ship. On stepping onto the car deck she was relieved to find that hers was the only one left – her old faithful Volvo. The deck hands complaining and signalling for her to hurry on. Throwing her bag into the back she fired up the engine and drove off onto British soil once more. As she neared the security sheds she rehearsed what she was going to say. Slowing down to join the queue – something caught her eye – a silver jeep had pulled alongside her and once again she saw the glint, smile and a finger raised to silence lips.

Twenty years had passed and the longer she had left it – the more impossible it became for her to report. For months afterwards every time a streak of silver from a passing vehicle came into view – the familiar trembling would instinctively kick in. She had scoured the papers for news of the missing man, but nothing. There was always talk of lads who had lost their way, boarding the ship but not arriving at their destination. An urban myth, she had previously thought, circulated by generations of emigrants. Around six months later she read an article about an Irish family trying to trace their son / brother who had

181

disappeared on a business trip to England – the same checked jacket peering out from the grainy photograph. She had lifted the phone a few times, only for the lasting image of the silencing silver jeep to cloud her thoughts.

Pounding the pavements now, she reflected on the toll the events that fateful evening had taken. Her promising career and relationship had crumbled to nothingness. She had isolated herself from family and friends and as time flittered away, their attempts at maintaining contact had dwindled. The bite of the snow had reduced to a softer sleet. She pulled out her phone from her pocket, stared at it and then began to press the digits. A silver streak caught her eye. She hung up.

Leaning against the slammed front door, she tried to control her breathing. In for seven out for eleven.... The life-affirming walk had shifted gear into a ragged run, which her body was not designed to undertake. Maintaining control was what got her through each day. When this slipped, the downward spiral began to spin. The self-destruct button was activated. With wobbly legs she approached the fridge. Scanning the contents she tried to find inspiration to tempt her empty stomach, but her eyes drifted to the inevitable bottle of chilled Pinot Grigio. ne glass just to steady herself and then she'd think of food. She'd put another one in, to chill.

'Beep, beep, beep,' the piercing noise increased, forcing her to lift her head from the velvet cushion, a trail of saliva like a line keeping the connection, seeped from the corner of her mouth. Head thumping competing with what she realised was the smoke alarm. Jumping up she collided with the coffee table and empty wine bottle en route to the oven. Upon opening revealed the remnants of her pasta bake supper. In disgust she watched the charred meal slide into the food bin. Back to the fridge, glad that she had thought to replace the bottle. As the wine hit the back of her throat she felt a slight calming, tipped down with two pain killers and a packet of crisps thrown into the mix. Mindlessly she flicked on the television. Numbness beginning to creep in, she watched what her mother would have called, 'inane drivel', the reality TV show preventing her mind from going into melt down. It hurt to think of her parents, a gut-wrenching ache, but she had distanced from them for a reason. She was contemplating going to bed when she heard the familiar introduction to the news.

'Today marks the twentieth anniversary of .... His family knew that he planned to travel to the
North-West of England on business .... booked on the night ferry from Dublin to Holyhead...wearing a checked jacket ... A new witness has come forward who remembers seeing him in the bar area. Police are appealing for more new witnesses, who travelled to Holyhead that night...'

A new witness...? She couldn't think about it now. She'd check in the morning – she'd probably misheard. More wine would help to block out the lucid images re-running on a loop in her mind. It generally worked, although it took more than usual. She woke at 3:00 am, covered in sweat, with visions of her removing the blade from his chest, her mind playing tricks on her again. A black and white film was playing in the background. She knew she should climb the stairs for a decent sleep, but dragged the throw off the back of the couch wrapping it around her, holding tight the old Galway jersey.

Sleep evaded her conflicted mind. A new witness...? Questions repeatedly popped into her head. Who? Why now? Could this be the catalyst she needed to rid herself of the suffocating secret? Consequences? Could she be strong enough? Would the man's family forgive her? Was there a chance she could have saved his life? If only she had someone to confide in. She had come close a few times but terror maintained her silence. And yet she realised that she couldn't continue to live her life in a state of paranoia, triggered each time she glimpsed a silver car. Dawn began to creep through the gap in the curtains.

'After twenty years of waiting the family of a missing Irish man maybe a step closer to finding out what happened to their beloved son and brother... New information has come to light and in a joint operation with the Garda Síochána and North Wales Police, Greater Manchester Police are keen to trace the owner of a red Volvo 440 from the night of....'

She watched eyes widening in disbelief as the news broadcast programme cut to a police spokesperson. 'We are also interested in making contact with a woman who today would most likely be in her forties. A brief description has been circulated, long dark hair, green eyes and was possibly wearing a GAA/sports jersey on the night in question. Although we do appreciate that memories are not as clear after such a lapse of time and naturally appearances will have changed. Anyone with information should get in touch with ...'

This couldn't be happening. Her mind couldn't comprehend. How? Why? After all this time – he had finally got to her. The witness had become the suspect. She clung onto the blood-stained jersey.

Author's note: I have been travelling back and forth to Ireland on the ferry for family holidays, with my parents and siblings and later with my husband and children, for as long as I can remember. It is a shared experience with countless second-generation children and part of growing up in an Irish family. These journeys along with urban myths regarding people disappearing and not disembarking, were the starting point for this short story.

PREVIOUS PUBLICATIONS

In addition to *Life and Soul* the Manchester Irish Writers have published six other books.

At The End of the Rodden (1997) is a collection of stories and poetry edited by Sean Body and launched by Aine Moynihan, theatre director, actor and writer, An Lab Theatre, Dingle.

The Retting Dam is a collection of poetry, edited by Stella-Marie Hinchcliffe and Alrene Hughes and officially launched by Polly Devlin OBE at the Manchester Irish Festival 2001.

A Stone of the Heart (2002) is a collection of short stories edited by Stella-Marie Hinchcliffe and Alrene Hughes.

Drawing Breath, is a collection of monologues, first performed by the Manchester Irish Writers in the Royal Exchange Theatre in September 2003.

Changing Skies is a collection of monologues, first performed at the Irish World Heritage Centre in March 2014, to mark the twentieth anniversary of the Manchester Irish Writers, edited by Alrene Hughes and Kevin McMahon, and published by PublishNation.

For information on these publications and their availability contact Rose Morris:
rose@altmore.com.

In addition, *Kerry Child to Limerick Lady* (2004) is the late Ida Kennelly's autobiography, edited by her daughter, Manchester Irish Writer, Marion Riley. This book brings together a collection of memoirs and photographs that Manchester Irish Writer, Marion Riley, found after the death of her mother Ida Kennelly. It is a very moving and honest account providing a vivid and revealing story of a Kerry childhood during the War of Independence and Civil War in Ireland, the flight to the sanctuary of England and subsequent return to settle in Limerick. This work was published by *Scribhneoiri*, the Manchester Irish Writers' own publishing company (whose title comes from the Irish word for "writers").

For information regarding this book and its availability, contact Marion Riley: rileytirdfloor@aol.com

The Manchester Irish Writers were also featured in *Something About Home: New Writing on Migration and Belonging,* edited by Liam Harte (Geography Publications, 2017)

scríbhneoirí